PRAISE FOR *POWERED BY HAPPY*

"*Powered by Happy* provides a step by step, tip by tip strategy for figuring out what gives us joy and how to create an environment in which we can find it—all day, every day, in any situation, no matter what challenges we face."

—Larry Israelite, talent management executive

"Beth Thomas has creatively added happiness to the list of key competencies for personal and organizational effectiveness. Here is a practical collection of strategies and approaches that will support and enliven the lives of employees and managers."

—Elliott Masie, chair, The Learning Consortium

"Look hard into the mirror, be honest with yourself, follow Beth's advice, and become more productive and *honestly happy!*"

—Steven M. Lyman, vice-president,
American Eagle Outfitters

"I recommend this read for anyone looking to boost success."

—Jonathan M. Kayes, chief learning officer,
Central Intelligence Agency

"In *Powered by Happy*, Beth Thomas reminds us that we're supposed to be happy and gives us some important tools to keep us on track. Happy people actually create more productive and profitable workplaces where people are able to show up as their best selves. A meaningful read for business leaders along with parents trying to develop happy children."

—Betsy Myers, former COO, Obama for America Presidential Campaign, and former executive director of Harvard's Kennedy School Center for Public Leadership

POWERED BY HAPPY

POWERED BY HAPPY

How to Get and Stay Happy at Work

(BOOST PERFORMANCE, INCREASE SUCCESS,
AND TRANSFORM YOUR WORKDAY)

Beth Thomas

Published by Sourcebooks, Inc.
P.O. Box 4410, Naperville, Illinois 60567-4410
(630) 961-3900
Fax: (630) 961-2168
www.sourcebooks.com

Library of Congress Cataloging-in-Publication Data

Thomas, Beth.
  Powered by happy : how to get and stay happy at work (boost performance, increase success, and transform your workday) / Beth Thomas.
      p. cm.
  Includes bibliographical references.
  1. Job satisfaction. 2. Employee motivation. 3. Work and family. 4. Happiness.
I. Title.
  HF5549.5.J63T49 2010
  650.1—dc22

                                2009039229

Printed and bound in the United States of America.
VP 10 9 8 7 6 5 4 3 2

This book is dedicated to the people most responsible for making me a happy person. First, the most phenomenal parents ever, Jack and Mary Jean Comas, who were taken from us far too young, provided me the lifelong love, support, and teachings that made me the happy person I am today. In addition, my darling family, who have helped me grow and sustain that happiness every day: my husband, J. T., who is my best friend and the love of my life, and my precious little angels, Tiffany Nicole and Madison Leigh. From the moment I looked into their eyes, I felt a love greater than one could ever imagine. Each of them has brought me more happiness than they will ever know. They are the light of my life and bring sunshine into my every day. Finally, all my many special sisters, friends, in-laws, and colleagues whom I have been so blessed with in my life: thank you for all you do to help me be happy.

It is with much admiration and sadness that I also dedicate this book to my best friend in the world, Sue Schwanenberger LeClair, who lost her long and courageous battle to cancer on April 18, 2009. She was my hero, and much of my happiness throughout my life is attributable to her.

CONTENTS

INTRODUCTION

Are you happy?

How you answer that question probably depends on what area of your life you think about first. Your spouse? Home? Children? Friends? Work?

For most people, work isn't the first thing that comes to mind. But a lack of happiness at work can have a huge impact. When you are unhappy at the office, that feeling overflows into every part of your life. On the flip side, when you are happy in your nine-to-five, that joy pervades every area of your life. Unfortunately, happiness can sometimes play a serious game of hide-and-seek.

I'm not telling you anything you don't know—at least not yet. We all know how difficult it can sometimes be to find joy at work, whether you're in a cubicle or a corner office. And we all know, in a vague, rainbows-and-butterflies way, that more happiness in the hallways at work would be good.

But it's a little more serious than that. True happiness improves the bottom line—yours and your company's.

Don't believe me? Research at the Wharton School at the University of Pennsylvania has shown that U.S. corporations with the happiest employees have a financial performance notably better than lower-ranked companies. Why is this? Common sense might offer hints, but other happiness research proves it: people who are happy function better, according to folks like happiness expert Alexander Kjerulf. Happy associates are productive associates.

And being happy at work is more important for *you* than most people think. Why? Because being happy at work is the first step in a sequence that leads to success. If you are happy at work, you become engaged in your work. If you are engaged, increased productivity, better results, and stronger relationships with your co-workers will follow. Happiness can not only skyrocket your career, but it can also transform your every workday. What's more, being happy not only affects your work; it affects your entire life in a positive way. Who wouldn't want that?

Not just working professionals. A positive psychology class nicknamed Happiness 101, taught by professor Tal Ben-Shahar, recently beat out Intro to Economics as the most popular course at Harvard, with more than 850 students enrolled in its last offering. In the last several years, positive psychology courses have popped up on over a hundred campuses around the country. These classes aim to better prepare young adults by teaching them that you do not just need the technical knowledge of how to move ahead in your career; happiness plays a significant role in your overall success as a professional and a person. And people want to learn how to get happy.

My hunch is that because we spend so much time occupied in our jobs and careers, achieving happiness at work goes a long way toward finding overall happiness.

"That's great and all," I can hear you saying, "but how do I get happy at work? How can I harness happy as the fuel that runs my days?"

You're about to find out. *Powered by Happy* is a pocket-sized blueprint that shows you how office happiness is accessible to anyone. It's as easy as taking the time to train for it. That may sound a little nuts, but think about it this way: If you want to learn a new computer skill, you train for it. If you want to learn a new presentation skill, you train for it. If you want to learn to be happy during your day job—you've come to the right place.

It's not true that happiness comes only to those who were born with a naturally positive attitude or to those who have lots of money and plenty of good luck. It can be yours as well; you just need to cultivate it. Inside this book, you'll find the tools you need to be happy every day. Not just a book of rah-rah rhetoric that gives you a big, sugary high of optimism only to leave you cold hours later, *Powered by Happy* offers techniques and tips to give you more personal freedom, a more positive feeling, deeper fulfillment, and less stress, regardless of your life or work circumstances.

That said, we all know there is plenty around us that can threaten to crush happiness.

Ironically, just days after I penned the final chapter of this little book on happiness, I found myself in a state of profound sadness. After a nine-year battle with breast cancer, my best and dearest childhood friend—someone who had been with me during some of the happiest moments of my life—passed away. Alone in a hotel room, hours after delivering her eulogy in front of her three young sons, husband, and parents, I wept inconsolably.

If ever there was a time to employ my own advice about seeking and finding happiness, it was then. The work I knew I would have to do following the loss of such a joyous person in my life was, in many ways, the very reason I wrote this book.

The bed of roses, the bowl of cherries—we all know they don't just appear every morning when we get up. If your life is anything like mine, it's better described by words like "roller coaster" and "yo-yo." I've dealt with the twists, the turns, the challenges, and the disappointments. I was not born of privilege, and I am certainly not lucky. I've been hired, fired, celebrated, and abused by bosses in my work life. And at home

I've had to work just as hard as others to keep my marriage and my two kids on the right track.

I learned a long time ago that if you are to achieve true happiness in your life, you must attack it with passion, discipline, and courage. You have to want it. And it's work. But do the work, and you will realize rewards beyond what you can imagine.

Years ago, I discovered another passion in my life. It was helping companies teach and train employees to be truly satisfied in their jobs. I was an employee engagement expert, if you will. In my first job as a corporate trainer, I saw firsthand the sheer pleasure people got from getting better at something. It didn't matter what that something was. I knew this was the career for me, and over the years, I have had the pleasure of motivating and helping thousands of employees, managers, and CEOs to advance their skills. I've been instrumental in turning around productivity at Limited Brands through training and development, as well as supporting major transformations at Bank One and JPMorgan Chase. I have had the pleasure of consulting in great companies such as American Eagle Outfitters and DSW, where I have helped lead organizational redesigns and transformations in the business. In each circumstance, I have become friends with the leaders who ran these companies as well as the individual contributors who executed the work every day. In the process, I learned about what great leaders do to make their associates happy, and what can happen when their associates feel and respond to those efforts.

I've shown these friends and some of America's top organizations how happy associates are productive associates and how they can develop these happy—and thus committed—employees. Now, I thought, why not motivate and help others to advance their own happiness?

All the secrets to my success in finding happiness at work are included in this book. It's a summary of best practices that will help not only company workers but also company leaders—those who can light the way to creating a culture of happy and engaged associates.

Perhaps this is why my book is different from others that offer self-help. It is less theory and more training manual. I'm no scholar, but I know how to help people practice and learn how to get what they want.

A few years ago, I was the keynote speaker at an industry conference. I was frankly surprised by the throng of people who gathered around the stage to meet and chat when my session was over. "How do you stay so upbeat?" one woman asked. Another remarked, "Are you always this happy? It seems to come so naturally to you!"

Little did they know how hard I have worked to achieve the joy and gratitude I feel today. In this book, I share many of my own stories, experiences, and habits that have led me to be able to make the statement "I am truly happy in my life."

I wasn't, however, just born happy. I have learned to be happy. I have trained for it all my life. I know how to create a plan. I don't just talk theory; I talk real life. The reason I have excelled in my career as a training and change-management expert is that I love sharing what I have learned with others and seeing them reach their potential. And now I want to do the same for you.

I've translated my two decades of experience into a personal coaching program—a kind of road map to happiness—for readers who feel trapped, stymied, and stuck. *Powered by Happy* is deliberately a small book, filled with ten chapters of useful tips and tricks. You'll find upbeat coaching, worksheets, checklists, and practical lessons that can be put into action today. Each chapter will introduce the benefits of the lesson for a happier life and will incorporate exercises, lists of tips, challenging questions and suggestions, and specific action steps for you to implement immediately. I've tucked in lots of stories that will make you laugh and cry, and make each lesson real, achievable, and inspiring. I have also polled colleagues, experts, business owners, and friends for valuable input, advice, and opinions to share.

It's important to note that many of these friends are top leaders and individual contributors from Fortune 500 companies. Many of them started out as clients, but over the course of twenty years in corporate America, many have become my friends. And now they're sharing their wisdom with you.

So where do we start? First, I'll share how to create your own definition of happiness. Chapter 1 challenges the myths of what makes you really happy and includes step-by-step instructions for creating a specific definition of what happiness means to you. Chapter 2 is about learning to choose happiness, to reprioritize your approach to being happy. That includes coping with the hard stuff and finding out how to own your attitude. In chapter 3, you'll learn how to break down barriers that stand in the way of your happiness. This chapter explains how worry, distorted thinking, and replaying negative stories in your mind can derail your plans to be happier and more fulfilled. In chapter 4, you'll learn how to build a support team of people who get it—and get rid of everyone else. And if you're the type who's always making a to-do list, chapter 5 shows you how to replace it with something even bigger. In chapter 6, you'll discover ways to take the "un" out of "unhappy," and you'll learn why being grateful has so much to do with it. Chapter 7 tackles the biggest investment you can make in your own happiness—and it might surprise you—and chapter 8 spells out ways to make happiness as much of a routine as your morning coffee. In chapter 9, you'll discover a no-fail strategy to upping your happiness, and in chapter 10, we'll wrap it up by looking at even more ways to inject some joy into your workday.

WHY COMPANIES SHOULD CARE ABOUT WORKPLACE HAPPINESS

I have done several studies on happiness in the workplace through my personal MHCS (Master Human Capital Strategist) certification. Through this process, I was trained on how important talent development and happiness are to the bottom line. It's clear that they should be above anything else the leadership team works on. The Human Capital Institute has actually stated that 70% of a leader's job should focus on building talent and creating an engaging culture.

It will pay off: Sears Roebuck can prove that a 5% increase in employee commitment will drive a 1.8% increase in customer commitment, which yields a .5% increase in financial returns.

Conversely, when associates are not happy or engaged in their work, it will *cost* your company! A national survey by *Gallup Management Journal* found that disengaged associates cost the U.S. economy more than $300 billion a year in lost productivity, higher turnover, and diminished business success.

This is so important that I'm going to say it again: companies benefit when their associates are happy. It is critical that leadership take happiness into account, as it forms the culture in which the company's associates work. Whether the economy is up or down, whether it's an "employee market" or "employer market," building a good culture at work should be the top initiative of every company.

I have seen many leaders in a down economy lose their perspective on the importance of employee satisfaction. I've heard managers say flippant things like, "Let them leave. Where are they going to go?" and "There are no jobs out there, and we can replace them in a minute." People who have this kind of attitude hurt their company in more ways than one. Not only do they refuse to remedy the problem that is causing their employees to look for other work, but they also make their employees feel inferior.

But the worst thing these managers do is send the message that they don't value the talent of their employees. When the market gets better, the talented employees will be the first to go, because they will remember the way their managers talked about them. Talent is the source of a company's strategic advantage. You have to take care of that talent in good times and in bad by creating a culture in which employees can thrive and be productive.

When employees are scared they are going to lose their jobs if they don't put in sixty-hour work weeks, they're wasting their energy on negative thoughts when they could be producing. Working harder doesn't mean working smarter; many times it is the opposite. I have so many friends who put in extra hours just for face time. This is a bad habit and a bad management tactic. Taking care of your associates will always help you in the long run. They will be much more loyal and much more productive, which will ultimately increase your bottom line and shareholder value.

The way that companies perceive their employees is changing—and that's a good thing. Gone are the days when managers ruled with an iron fist, yelled at their reports, and dominated through intimidation. With the younger, more creative and energetic generations entering the workforce, managers are realizing that trust and respect are the most important tools for creating strong and dynamic corporate environments.

The material in *Powered by Happy* can be applied at work or at home. What is important to you at work will absolutely affect you at home and in other areas of your life. These days, our worlds of personal and professional life have become more homogeneous than ever, and when you can achieve happiness in one area, you'll find it spreading to the other area of your life. So why not have techniques that allow more happiness and satisfaction to spill into both?

And so I give unto you this little gift of happiness. Make this book your own. Write notes in it and use it as your personal training guide as you go through your own challenges. I hope it leads you to all the things you've ever wanted out of life. Enjoy.

:)

CREATE YOUR OWN DEFINITION OF HAPPINESS

Over the years, I've noticed that the topic of happiness sparks a lot of curiosity and plenty of interesting conversation. Perhaps it's because the very thing that has such potential to enrich our everyday existence is also the one thing that eludes so many of us.

I think part of the reason happiness often seems out of reach is that we don't take the time to really figure out what will make us happy.

For me, happiness is waking up and feeling like every day is Christmas, feeling excited and blessed to live another day among my family and friends. To appreciate life, to love, and to laugh is my way of living because it spills over into the workplace, where, for better or worse (and I prefer "better"), I spend most of my waking hours.

So what about you? When you're happy, can you actually articulate the reasons why? That is, can you define what will make you happy?

HAPPINESS NOTE CARD: FRIENDS DONATE THEIR HAPPINESS DEFINITIONS

I recently polled several friends and family members and asked them to share their definitions of true happiness:

- "Being with family—that could make me happy even if we didn't have a dime."

- "Making six figures by the time I am forty."

- "Starting my own business, making it successful, and then selling it—preferably to a company like Microsoft or Yahoo!"

- "Knowing I run a successful business that contributes to the happiness of my employees."

- "Living with my illness without bitterness and only gratitude."

- "The intangible feelings of deep faith, unconditional love, and a sense of accomplishment."

- "Good health—that's all I need to be happy."

- "Being at peace with myself."

- "Knowing I made a difference with my life."

- "Happiness is balance, love, family, friends, and challenge."

- "Helping my kids lead productive lives and contributing to society."

- "Hearing my kids laugh, having a great marriage."

- "A cool breeze on a summer night, the moon shining through the pines, and stars in the sky."

In this chapter, I'll challenge you to answer the question of what makes you happy and identify your own definition of happiness. If you're reading this book, then you know that those of us with careers sometimes spend more time at work than we do with the ones we love. We spend more time doing our work than doing the things we love most. For this reason, your definition of happiness should include how you will be happy at work. Knowing exactly what happiness means to you—not to your boss, your co-worker, your client, or anyone else (even those outside the workplace)—is like discovering the arrow on a compass. Suddenly, you'll become aware of the direction you really need to go.

I'm always surprised by how many people can't define happiness for themselves. Or how many of them define happiness in terms of possessions, material things, or things that are unrealistic or outside their reach. I'm all for dreams, but when you dream the impossible, you are likely to be disappointed. When creating my career goals, I took it one step at a time. I didn't expect to be a CEO right out of college. When defining happiness for yourself, remember this: keep it real, keep it meaningful, and keep it about yourself.

Sadly, I even talk to people whose happiness, especially at work, is obviously being defined by someone else. They feel bogged down by the need to please a demanding boss, to placate a meddlesome co-worker, or to pacify a temperamental client. There's no denying that showing loyalty to your employer, or loving and giving to others uncondition-ally, can be deeply satisfying. But someone else's happiness is rarely the secret to yours.

"I just want my kids to be happy so I can be happy," a colleague told me recently. But this is also someone who is constantly exhausted by the effort it takes to satisfy her chil-dren's many demands. Is she really experiencing true happi-ness? I doubt it. She, like many of us, needs a whole new definition of the term.

Of course, defining happiness doesn't make you happy, but it's an important step toward achieving what can bring true meaning to your life—and true satisfaction at work.

But have you looked around at work lately? What do you see written on the faces of your colleagues, your boss, or even your own team? I'd venture to say you're seeing a lot of furrowed brows and frowns. Let's back up and take a look at how they got there to begin with.

THERE'S NO "I" IN MONDAY MISERY

According to the Human Capital Institute, a staggering 75 percent of the millions of working Americans are not happy at their jobs.

Why are so many people unhappy? In my career, I have met people at all levels who believe their company is "screwing" them or that they are a victim of a bad situation at work. Those folks rarely think that the blame is two-sided.

They don't consider that perhaps they are not pulling their weight or contributing, that they have a part in the situation they're in. Does it make sense to define happiness as wanting to be the CEO of the company, but then to walk around with an attitude, complain, and never meet deadlines? Probably not. Being "powered by happy" at work means more than just defining what happiness means to you. It means having the courage to take charge of making it happen.

I'd like to share a story that illustrates what I'm talking about.

I was twenty-nine years old and on the fast track to a great career with an international brokerage firm. I had a loving husband, a beautiful three-year-old daughter, and a great job—talk about having it all! I loved my job. It was perfect for me and for my life, or so I thought. I was in charge of office administration, accounting, sales, and computer training and support. Sounds like a lot, but I loved it. It provided a challenge, professional development, and enough diversity that I never got bored. I was able to travel the world and see places that I never dreamed I would see. I worked with executives who were twice my age, three times my seniority level, and earning paychecks worth more than quadruple my dollar value. Again, life was good.

Then one night while traveling in England, I called to wish my three-year-old, Tiffany, a good night, and for the first time since I had her, she realized I was gone, really gone. Up until this point, my travel was her "vacation." She got to visit her grandmothers and was spoiled beyond belief. But even at three years old, she was getting wise enough to realize that her mom was not there to tuck her in at night. When I spoke with her, she started crying, "Mommy, come home! You no here—I need you here!" I was in such shock that I didn't know how to respond; nothing in my parenting books had taught me what to say or how to react. So I reacted by crying, too. I was devastated. All of a sudden, my perfect job—the job that helped make me happy and fulfilled—was now something that was coming between me and my happiness.

The last three days of my trip seemed to last forever, and I will never forget my trip home. I experienced a life-altering conversation with a complete stranger, a conversation that I live by to this day. I was sitting next to a man who noticed my preoccupation (and depression) and started chatting about being stuck in an airport. Half-listening, I was playing along, and as we bonded, I started to share my story of my distraught three-year-old and how horrible I felt when I heard her cry. Abruptly, he stopped me and said, "Listen, you seem like a bright young woman, but at the end of the day, nobody ever says they wished they'd worked more. They say they wished they had spent more time with their family. I hope you remember that as your daughter grows up and someday, very quickly, will be gone away to school and on to her own life."

Wow. Have I heard this kind of story before? Absolutely. At the exact moment I needed to hear it? Never!

Within a month of that conversation, I quit my job. Yes, the job I loved, the one that made me happy every day. However, what "having it all" meant to me had changed, and thank God it did, because my two beautiful girls will tell you that I have been there for them, in sickness and in health, ever since.

The ending of my story is a happy one. I took another job that provided the same level of challenge but with no travel. Who knows? At another point in my life, I may go back to a job where I travel the world, and at that point, it may bring happiness to my life. But one thing is for certain, when your family is a big part of your happiness and your work is interfering with that, there is only one thing to do: take charge of your destiny, and change things to fit your life so you're happy at work and home.

Whether you are starting your career, in your midcareer, or ending your career, what happiness is to you varies, changes, and evolves. Your goals and definitions should be achievable and specific according to where you are right now. What is perfect one day can change the next day. You need to be agile and take full responsibility of making changes to your career that fit with *your* life at this time.

HOW TO DEFINE WHAT HAPPINESS MEANS TO YOU

It's a simple fill-in-the blank sentence.

"What makes me truly happy is _____."

Having done this exercise myself, I can tell you it's not as easy as it sounds. Why? Because most of us start with a list that's simply too long. We define happiness as "having it all."

HAVING IT ALL VS. HAVING WHAT YOU WANT

"Having it all" is a dreaded phrase women have heard for decades. Fueled by success in nearly every political, educational, and professional arena we've played in over the last fifty years, we've discovered we have the potential to do incredible things. But with that potential comes lots of pressure. Living media-rich lives has added to that. We read money magazines and feel like we're falling behind financially. We see beautiful women in the fashion spreads and feel we aren't measuring up. We look at the picture-perfect families featured in parenting magazines and feel like failures.

That's why I recommend redefining what "having it all" means to you. Good health or simple financial stability might be all you need. Maybe it's having a win every day at work, whether it is a compliment from your boss or a colleague or checking off all your to-dos for the day. A great family can supply all the reasons you feel genuinely happy every day. All-consuming happiness might come simply from excelling at a hobby or activity you've always wanted to master. Maybe it comes down to resetting your expectations just a bit.

We are living in a world of abundance. So many people perceive each other's happiness in terms of wealth or status. At work, we often think that those who sit in the biggest offices with the most prestigious titles must be the happiest. But try looking at it another way: How many people do you know who are unhappy because their cleaning lady came two days late, or their pool boy didn't show up over the weekend, or they lost several thousand dollars in an overinflated stock market, or their child didn't get into that Ivy League college? How do you perceive wealth, status, and possessions? Do they substantially affect your happiness?

I can't say it enough (and I will many times in this book): long-term, sustained happiness at home or work does not come from money or things. It comes from a state of being, from feeling good about helping others, from your attitude and how you deal with unpleasant things, from understanding what happiness means to you, and from setting realistic expectations.

As you can tell, I'm a real believer in taking control of your own happiness. But your life can't be powered by happy if you don't know what happiness means for you. Think about the world's most successful leaders, our

MY DEFINITION OF HAPPINESS

- Being a good Christian with a giving heart
- Being a good wife and mother
- Being a good friend
- Having a meaningful and successful career

country's most successful corporate executives, or even the most successful parents you know. They all have goals they can clearly and simply articulate, if asked. They may certainly rely at times on feelings and intuition, but they also have a defined plan for success. You too can apply these same rules for success and achieve a lot more happiness at the office, as well as in other areas of your life.

Think of the assignment to write your own simple definition of happiness as the start of something great. Right there on paper, staring back at you, will be the very things that have the potential to give your life new and greater meaning. Sometimes you may have more than one definition of happiness. You may have a definition for happiness that applies to all areas of your life, or you may get specific about what happiness means to you as a professional, parent, spouse, or friend. Here are some things to think about as you embark on this important process:

GUIDELINE #1: YOUR HAPPINESS DEFINITION SHOULD FOCUS ON THINGS THAT WILL MAKE YOU HAPPY FOR A LONG TIME

Things like money, sports cars, new clothes, a fancy house, or even winning the lottery are only going to sustain your happiness for so long. I compare these things to gorging on a big dessert or eating a giant chocolate bar. Think about what happens when you eat a sugary treat. You get that great sugar high for a few hours and then crash into a food coma. The feeling simply doesn't last.

Contrast that feeling to how you feel when you help a colleague in need, teach your direct report an important skill, comfort a grieving co-worker, achieve a significant goal you've worked hard and long for, or do someone a big favor. Many actions contribute to being happy that have nothing to do with short-term material goods. Think about this important principle as you write your own definition of happiness. It will help you balance your happiness at work.

GUIDELINE #2: YOUR HAPPINESS DEFINITION CAN HAVE MULTIPLE COMPONENTS

If you look at the definition of happiness I've written for myself, you'll see it covers many areas of my life. There are times when I'm 100 percent focused on happiness with my family and times when I'm 100 percent focused on happiness at work. Okay, I admit it: I also sometimes spend 100 percent of my time curled up on the couch! This is no problem— your road to happiness can have many footpaths, trails, and thoroughfares. It might span the topics of family, friends, faith, career, hobbies, health, or community service. Don't make your happiness list too vague, but don't be afraid to seek happiness in different, specific, and unusual ways.

Rather than thinking of things that make you happy, think of actions instead. What do you do that makes you happy? Perhaps it's that monthly volunteer work at your local YWCA/YMCA to mentor young people trying to make a better life for themselves. Or maybe it's finding a new hobby, taking a course at a local college, mentoring a colleague you see struggling at work, or mentoring a young professional.

GUIDELINE #3: YOUR HAPPINESS DEFINITION SHOULD REFLECT YOUR DREAMS BUT ALSO BE ACHIEVABLE

Of course, I think a chance to represent my country in the Olympics would make me really happy. My happiness quotient would soar if I knew no child in the world had to go hungry. And nothing would make me happier than to be able to hug my late parents just one more time. The reality is, some things you and I might include in a definition of happiness are simply out of reach. I'm not suggesting you scale back on ambitious expectations—dream big and go for it!—but do so within reason. You would have to agree that, for me, being a better golfer is far more achievable than counting on a trip to the Olympics. I can do a lot of good for hungry kids by volunteering at our local food bank. And I can remember my wonderful parents every day by keeping my favorite pictures close and sharing the many gifts they taught me about the importance of family. That's a lot of happiness, and it's all within my reach.

Let's take this guideline to work. Each one of us has dreams of where we would like to see our careers go. Some goals may be simple, some ambitious, and some just flat-out unrealistic. When considering dreams at work, complete this sentence:

> "At the end of my career, if I accomplished [fill in goal here], I would be satisfied."

That goal could be a certain position, an occupation, a salary figure, or a combination of all three. It could also be centered on a certain lifestyle or culture.

Let me share my personal goal with you. When I was thirty-five, I set my career goal as follows: "I want to quit working for someone else at fifty-five. I want to then own my own consulting firm, work two days a week, and make at least six figures doing so."

In order to achieve this goal, I had to work backward and figure out what skills, knowledge, and abilities it would take for me to get there, as well as what it would take financially. I learned I would have to have all my debt paid off (house and car) and put my kids through college. I would have to diversify my background and gain experience in the consulting field. Three years after I turned thirty-five, I met with a financial planner and created a plan for how to reach my financial goals. I then realized my background needed to be more diversified, and I changed industries while enhancing my skill set. Finally, I took a position within an organization running its management-consulting division. Just working toward my goals has taken a lot of planning and ambition. But because they were realistic goals, I could figure out the numerous smaller steps they required. If I had said I wanted to be the president of GM, make seven figures, and retire by the age of fifty, I'm pretty sure I would have set myself up for a personal failure, which, by the way, never makes you feel happy.

SOME MORE INSPIRATION FOR YOU

I polled a few clients, colleagues, and friends who have helped shape my career and provided endless hours of great advice when I needed it most. Here are some of their thoughts on how to be happy at work. I was struck by how often their answers hit on similar themes:

- The freedom of owning my own business, knowing that every choice I make is a direct reflection on my business
- The ability to transfer knowledge to my clients as we move through a project
- Reflecting on how much I've learned and grown over my career
- Interacting with my co-workers
- The sense of accomplishment
- Being thanked
- Feeling like part of a team
- Having a boss who I know will support me and back me up no matter what

- Being challenged
- Helping the company grow
- Giving guidance and expertise in my area of knowledge
- Working without being micromanaged
- Achieving goals
- Being profitable
- Making my bonus
- Having an impact
- Feeling like what I do really makes a difference
- Creating something new or better than what has been done before
- Influencing others to share my passion or point of view
- Having fun
- Getting involved in our community through work
- Knowing that my efforts are making a positive difference
- Knowing that I will be rewarded for doing a good job
- Working in a positive environment...especially when donuts are involved
- Truly enjoying what I do
- Feeling appreciated
- Doing meaningful work
- Being included on significant assignments
- Doing work that challenges my skills and ability

THOUGHT-STARTERS: A SAMPLE LAUNDRY LIST OF HAPPINESS ATTRIBUTES

So we're back to that simple sentence, "What makes me truly happy is _____." If you're stuck on how to start creating a personal definition of happiness, here's a list to help you brainstorm. Think about each topic; then jot down thoughts that come to mind. Sort through your notes at the end, and rank them in order of importance. Don't forget that you can add items to this list, too. Remember that your point in time is important. When I first started working, my definition of happiness at work was to make as much money as I was years old. For example, when I was twenty-five, I wanted to make $25K. (This isn't my goal now.)

- **Family life:** What about your family life would make you happy? A great marriage? More fun or more time together? Even more kids? For your spouse or kids to understand the value of hard work? For them to look up to your work ethic and understand you work hard for them as well?

- **Relationships:** Are you a people person? Is the way you interact with others important to your happiness? What kind of person do you want to be? What qualities do you want to be known for in your relationships? How are your relationships at work? Do you foster collaboration? Do you work well with all levels in the organization? If you are a senior professional, do you look down on or disvalue the contributions of those below you?

- **Favorite activities and hobbies:** What activities really put you "in the zone" of happiness? What are the things you absolutely love to do? Would your happiness be furthered if you could add a new hobby or activity to the list? What things at work are you passionate about? What part of your job or your everyday tasks makes you the most happy?

- **Education:** What do you love to learn? What educational goals would make you happy? Will helping educate others contribute to your own happiness? How can you spend time coaching others in your organization? How can you take your education and experience and help those who are seeking advice or mentoring?

- **Health:** What are your goals for a healthy life, physically and emotionally? What makes you feel great? What does work/life balance mean to you? Is it working out every day at the office? Talking a walk outside to get rid of stress?

- **Personal and professional network:** How do the people around you contribute to your happiness? What's important to you in building and maintaining relationships across all aspects of your life? Think about where you can be happier at work, in your neighborhood, at church, or in your community. How can you network with others in your field? How do you connect with other professionals to keep your network current? This is a critical element to your future success as a professional.

- **Personal achievements:** Can you achieve greater happiness for yourself through any specific personal goals, such as overcoming an obstacle or excelling at something? It can be as simple as getting better at managing your time or keeping things neat around the house. How can you set specific goals at work that you can achieve? What are the attributes at work of the people who win "Star of the Year" awards? How can you be the next winner?

- **Financial:** What financial goals make you happy? How much money do you need to make? Want to make? How much do you deserve based on your level of contribution and added value to your business? You shouldn't expect to get paid more based on your tenure; it should be based on the value you add to the business and your personal performance.

- **Professional success:** Is achieving a set of goals at a paid or unpaid job a key to your happiness? If so, in what ways? What would make you happy professionally? Does being a great boss or a great employee define happiness for you? Remember to think about where you are in your career, and create professional goals from that vantage point.

- **Community:** Does giving to others and to your community give you a happy feeling? Think about the specific kinds of activities that make you feel that way. As a professional, especially at a senior level, you are expected to be philanthropic in your work. In my company, anyone in a leadership position is expected to be part of a nonprofit board. I am on the board of the American Red Cross Blood Division. It gives me great happiness to know that the experience and skills I have developed over the years can be utilized and valued by this critical organization.

Now, how do all these answers come together into a simple but personal happiness definition? I tried this on a friend recently. Here's what he wrote:

"What makes me truly happy is to have fun with everything I do and not sweat the small stuff. I love rebuilding old cars because it challenges me mentally and physically. I stay happy at work by trying to see the humor in things instead of getting stressed out about things I can't control. Improving my skill level at work, at home, and with my hobbies really makes me happy, so I work on those things all the time. Having fun with my family also makes me happy, and the joy I feel with them seems to have the same effect on them. These will always continue to be my goals for leading a happy life."

Great stuff, huh? I'd say he's well on his way to even more happiness in his life because his definition is clear.

But what if the picture isn't so rosy for you right now? What if you're unhappy? Can defining happiness help? I think so.

Here's a friend whose life struggles caused her to pause and rethink her definition of happiness. She wrote:

> *"I believe I can work my way back to happiness by letting go of some of the things that don't make me happy. I can't change the fact that I am now divorced. I need to stop trying to be all things to all people. Happiness for me would be developing a new hobby (I've always wanted to learn to refinish furniture) and getting really good at it without constantly feeling I'm stretched for time and can't fit it in. I would be happier if my kids were more self-sufficient, and that's something to work on. Finally, I've realized I need to return to my faith, because I think it would help me find some spiritual renewal and end the bitterness."*

I was truly inspired by this particular definition. Why? Because my friend had the courage to consider not only the things that could contribute to a happier life but also the things that were robbing her of it.

EXERCISE: DEFINE WHAT WILL MAKE YOU HAPPY NOW

Remember the tips I've given you here:

- Change your view of what it means to "have it all."

- Don't define your happiness strictly through the happiness of others.

- Don't just include material things or things that offer only short-term happiness.

- Consider what is sustainable over the course of your entire life.

- Think about what makes you happy in all aspects of your life.

STEP ONE

Using just a few words, list some of the items that define happiness for you:

_____

_____

_____

_____

STEP TWO

Using items from your list above, write a narrative description of what happiness means to you, similar to the example on page 9:

MY HAPPINESS DEFINITION

_____

_____

_____

_____

_____

_____

Well, you've just taken the first big step. You took charge of your own happiness and set a course for yourself. Now it's time to help you break down the barriers to achieving what you and you alone define as happiness. But remember, it's not just about *defining* happiness; it's also about *achieving* happiness and putting your definition into action.

HAPPINESS P.S.

A fine American essayist we all studied in school is associated with one of the best known happiness definitions. You'll probably recognize it. I've included it here for you to enjoy.

"To laugh often and much, to win the respect of intelligent people and affection of children, to earn the appreciation of honest critics and endure the betrayal of false friends, to appreciate beauty, to find the best in others, to leave the world a bit better whether by a healthy child, a garden patch, or a redeemed social condition, to know even one life has breathed easier because you have lived. This is to have succeeded."
—Ralph Waldo Emerson

:)

CHOOSE HAPPINESS AND MAKE IT HAPPEN

Are you in need of some happiness rehab?

Join the club! The world is an unhappy place these days. Every time I turn on the TV, all I see is misery. The worst financial crisis in history. Job losses at an all-time high. The fallout of an economic downturn that nobody knows how to deal with. Every time I read the paper, I see murders, burglaries, companies going bankrupt, and pictures of the homeless. Every day, I hear about unhappiness and tragedies from my own family and friends. Even movies are depressing. So with all this negativity surrounding us, how in the world are we supposed to find happiness?

HAPPINESS NOTE CARD: WHAT MY PARENTS TAUGHT ME ABOUT HAPPINESS— EVEN AFTER THEY WERE GONE

Sometimes we don't realize how smart our parents were until they are gone. After my parents died, I reflected on the lessons they taught me through their words and actions. They taught me that happiness is a choice and that happiness is what you make out of life. They taught me that happiness is turning lemons into lemonade every day and minimizing all the things that make you unhappy. They taught me that happiness comes from looking at every situation and making the best of it.

Have I had a good life? Absolutely! Have I had a tough life? You bet. The reason I'm a happy person today is that I made the most of those tough times, and now you can, too.

In this chapter, you'll learn to reprioritize your approach to happiness. You'll find out how to own your attitude and learn to cope with the hard stuff. And you'll hear from some of the happiness pros.

DOES HAPPINESS JUST HAPPEN?

Have you ever noticed how much time we spend talking about being unhappy? Now compare that to the time you spend discussing your happiness with others. I'll bet I know which subject takes up more of your time.

Unfortunately, learning to focus your energy on happiness instead of unhappiness isn't easy. Nope, it's something we have to work at.

Happiness isn't something that just happens. Happiness is how you deal with the cards you've been dealt. True, some of us are born with more of what I would call "happiness DNA," but there is more to being happy than just a naturally cheerful disposition.

It's not just about smiling all the time; it's about truly understanding what happiness means to you and utilizing this understanding to deal with every situation, every day. Each one of us has our own struggles, and a few of those struggles cause us to wonder if we will ever get through.

Think about how this applies at work. It takes time to move up, to get promoted, and to get recognized for your accomplishments. You have to work at being successful; it doesn't just happen. It is a choice. You choose to work, you choose to make goals for yourself, and you choose to work hard to achieve those goals. It's the same for achieving happiness. It's a choice, and it takes work. Working to be happy—it sounds counterintuitive, doesn't it? But if you work to be happy, you'll be happy at work.

I have a client who is an executive in information systems. Her boss's boss was an incredible leader and a huge fan of hers. Her business partner at work was also a huge fan. With these two champions in her corner, she was very happy. Then one day recently, both of her fans moved into different areas of the company. She suddenly realized that she had been dependent on their reactions and their praise of her work. Her happiness at work flowed from her colleagues, not from her—they were defining her happiness. This was a dangerous place to be, as when they left, her happiness took a huge hit. At first, she wanted to leave. However, after a short time, she realized that she just needed to switch things around a bit, to get a new perspective.

She spent time building new relationships, not only with her new leadership and business partners but, more importantly, with colleagues she had worked with for years but never taken the time to get to know. These new relationships helped ease the loss of the old ones and offered friendships and valuable sounding boards from people who knew the work she did and who could give her great advice. She also did a lot of soul searching to understand why specifically she was unhappy. She realized it was only partly because her biggest fans had left; it was also because she was a bit bored. She asked to take on more work, work that was directly aligned with the most critical project in the company. This action not only allowed her to become happy at work again but also created an opportunity to showcase her willingness, motivation, and value to the CEO and her boss. Now she is not dependent on anyone but herself to choose how she is happy at work. She owns her attitude.

I have managed many people throughout my career, and the ones who succeeded the most were the ones who had a great attitude. Their positivity was the catalyst for many, many promotions. Conversely, I have also had workaholic associates who took their bad attitudes to work. Unfortunately, their demeanor has led to several terminations.

When the importance of attitude is spelled out in these simple terms, it can be hard to understand how more people aren't doing everything they can to gain true happiness.

And sometimes you need to do a lot.

LEARNING TO FIND HAPPINESS THE HARD WAY

April 13, 1990, was the worst day of my life. I lost my hero, my dad, to cancer. After I heard that he had a cancer of "undetermined origin," I actually considered committing suicide for the first and only time in my life. It was devastating, and to this day I miss him more than words can say. Seven years later was the second worst day of my life. On that day, my dear mother was taken from us, also by cancer. Again, my world was turned upside down. She was my best friend, and my life will never be the same without her.

During this time in my life, I felt nearly overwhelmed by my grief. But I knew that the only way I could honor my parents' lives was to live a happy life myself.

So I tried as hard as I could to find a bright side in even the most heartbreaking events. After my dad died, I spent some time feeling angry that he wasn't with me anymore. I felt robbed that he'd been taken away. But then my aunt said something that helped me rearrange my perspective. She said, "You know, I had my dad for twice as long as you had yours. But the fifty years I had with my dad didn't even compare to the twenty-five years you had with your dad." And she was right. I learned to value the quality of my relationship with my father and be thankful for the time we had together. Then, when my mom died, I sank back into anger at God. This time, I knew I had to be the one to pull myself out of my misery, so I started to brainstorm about what positive things I could find in this situation. I thought about how maybe my mother's death was sparing her from something worse or how her death could have saved her from years of loneliness without my father. Thinking like this helped me see a sense of purpose in the events around me, and it taught me that even the worst situation can still be a lesson in gratitude.

At the same time that my mother was dying, I was selling my house, building a new house, dealing with a tumor I'd found in my breast (which I later learned was benign), learning of a precancerous mole on my eighteen-month-old daughter, and taking on the huge responsibility of managing Y2K training for all Limited Brands. I was basically dealing with every life stress, except for divorce (thank goodness), all at the same time. As if grief wasn't enough!

Again, I knew that if I wanted to get through each day, it

was going to take some work. In addition to finding a bright side in each situation, I started to play the "What's the worst-case scenario?" game with every problem that arose. This taught me two things: (1) to tackle one problem at a time in order to really evaluate what it represented; and (2) that even the worst outcome I could imagine was still something I could deal with. I also developed a strong support network of trusted friends who would listen to me, talk me off the ledge, and reassure me. My final strategy for coping with what seemed like insurmountable stress was probably the simplest, but it was definitely the most important: I prayed. And I gave my problems over to God.

Looking back, it was the toughest time in my life, and it taught me many things—but most of all, it taught me that no matter the tragedy, problem, or worry, I can get through it. Happiness is based on how you deal with the cards you have been dealt. You have a choice. You can let the cards get you down, or you can turn them over and just play your best game.

These stories may be personal, but each person has her own personal tragedies that wreak havoc on her career. That is why it is critically important that as you go through your own personal struggles, you remain focused on your job from nine to five, and then continue to work through your personal problems from five o'clock on. It's hard—trust me, I know—but some companies and some leaders don't have empathy for your non-work life. Plan time to focus on work and then time to focus on yourself.

Here are two time-tested principles that have changed the way I perceive my life and help me get through challenging situations.

EVERYTHING HAPPENS FOR A REASON

I left a fantastic job at Limited Brands to move to a new position at Bank One (now JPMorgan Chase) in 2003. I didn't want to leave the Limited; I loved it there. However, I felt that if I wanted to achieve my lifelong dream of being a consultant, or if having my own consulting business was going to come true, I needed to diversify my background. I spent two and a half years at Bank One, and it was a tough work environment. I actually questioned my decision to leave the Limited on many occasions. I thought I had made a bad decision and a bad career move. But then something funny happened. While I was at Bank One, I was recruited by my current employer, Sequent, to be the head of its consulting division. This is a job I would not have been as qualified for had I not diversified my background. I realized then, that as difficult as it had been, I needed to leave the Limited to grow and find the job I truly wanted. I am thankful that I made the decision, that it gave me more variety in my career, and that I ended up exactly where I wanted to be!

GOD IS TRYING TO TEACH US A LESSON HERE

When my mother was diagnosed with cancer, I was seven months pregnant with my daughter Madison. I will never forget when I heard the news; I fell to the ground and sobbed, "How could God do this to me?" So I came up with a simple plan: I was done with God. No more praying! No more faith! After taking my father from me, how could He take my mother? I was just pissed off!

That thinking lasted about a week. During that week, I was miserable. Not having God in my life was much more stressful than dealing with my mom's devastating news. By reacting selfishly to the news about my mom's cancer, I was making the situation worse for her and for me. Because abandoning my faith made me more stressed, it was harder for me to be there for my mom in her time of need. When I finally allowed myself to accept the news and ask for God's help, I was able to find comfort in prayer, and suddenly I could see that perhaps this was all part of a plan to help rather than hurt my family.

While I was going through all of these struggles at the same time, I actually threw myself into my work. It became part of my salvation. It not only enabled me to get a break from all my personal struggles, but it also made me a much stronger professional. You know the saying "What doesn't kill you makes you stronger." It was true in my case. Looking back, I can see that although I was going through a lot of personal struggles, I was also growing.

Another example in a business setting: I have a friend who is the CEO of a successful small business. He devoted his life to getting his company to the level that would provide a comfortable retirement for him and his family. The way he did this was to be intimately involved in the daily operations of his company. That worked well to a point, but it was taking over his life, making him work sixty to seventy hours per week. One day about six years ago, he found a lump on his neck. He soon discovered that it was a rare throat cancer. He had to take a leave of absence for six months and put the company in the hands of his management team. To him, his life was coming apart at the seams, but what he soon realized was that his company didn't need him as much as he thought it did. The operations still ran, the company still made money, and he was finally able to achieve a work/life balance. Ironically, the doctors thought his cancer might have been brought on by stress. After he quit working as much and started trusting the team he had put together, he was able to live in life a different, much happier way.

You too can find the happy in times of hardship. Here are some tips to help:

• **Be realistic, yet optimistic.** As my experiences have taught me, just wanting to be happy in tough times usually isn't good enough. You must have realistic expectations when trying to train yourself to be happy. There is only so much pressure you can put on yourself to make it happen. There are times when it's okay to be sad temporarily. For instance, when you lose a loved one or a job, when you have health issues, or when your children are hurt, you have to allow yourself the time to grieve or be sad. It's just a matter of how much time you give yourself. If you can create a plan and set expectations for your recovery, you'll find you might even be able to see what good can come out of the situation.

- **Own your attitude.** Know when you are not giving happiness a chance when you find yourself reacting negatively right away. When this happens, stop yourself and think of one positive thought. How many times at work does something happen that makes you want to scream? What do you do? Give in and scream? Yell? Throw dirty looks to the ones who "did this to you"? Pay them back on another project? Correct answer: none of the above. Rise above it. Take the high road. Never let them see you mad. It will always come back to bite you. You can tell them you disagree; you can ask for data or facts. But it's never a good idea to let your negativity flare out. I have never seen a "happy ending" when people do this. And think about this before you run to your colleague's desk to commiserate about how horrible your day is. Sure, we all need to vent, but make sure you're not making a toxic situation worse. Fanning the flames of a problem pushes your attitude in the wrong direction.

- **Look on the bright side.** It's there—you just have to find it. Have you ever heard, "Give them the benefit of the doubt"? You will hear more about this later in the book; however, happiness is largely about learned optimism. It is about training yourself to look on the bright side. In situations that get you down, turn it around by thinking of something good that will come out of the situation. There were times where I didn't get promoted quickly enough to the position I thought I deserved. Yet it always turned out to be the best thing for my career, allowing me to gain even more experience for an even bigger opportunity.

• **Play the "What's the worst-case scenario?" game.** This helps me a lot. There have been times when I would fret about something that, in the end, never materialized. It would have helped if I had thought, "What is the worst thing that could happen in this situation?" and figured out a way to deal with it. Just having that contingency plan in my pocket would have allowed me to move on.

• **Take one problem at a time**. How many times at work do your problems seem insurmountable? For me this happens when I'm when working with several different clients at a time. I take on their problems as my own, and suddenly I'm juggling too many different problems. Occasionally, it's too much, and I need to step back, write down the problems, prioritize them, and take them one at a time. As I work through one, it increasingly makes me feel better and motivates me to continue to solve the rest of them.

- **Develop a support network**. Create an alliance, populated by friends or colleagues or a mix of both whom you respect and value. The best way for me to get rid of my problems is to vent them to someone who understands what I am going through. The support and advice from friends over the years has saved me from years of misery and instead given me years of joy. For those of you who feel that sharing your problems is a tough thing to do, I urge you to start small with just one trusted friend. If you don't, you are not only missing out on great relationships that could play a huge part in your life but robbing yourself of happiness that is only a phone call away.

- **Pray or meditate.** Many folks are recharged by mentally retreating to a place of peace. Maybe it is visualizing yourself sitting on a beach or floating on a boat in the middle of the lake or resting in your place of worship. Whatever relaxes or calms you, find time to mediate, pray, and focus on all the good things in your life.

QUIT WAITING FOR HAPPINESS TO HAPPEN— GET GOING AND MAKE IT HAPPEN!

Just like almost everything else in our lives, self-improvement doesn't just happen. If I just want to lose five pounds, trust me, it won't work. If I just want that promotion, chances are it will pass me by. My point is that any self-improvement needs a plan. It needs work. Don't just sit and wait for happiness to come to you—go after it and get it. You're already well on the way. This book will teach you strategies that will help you increase your level of happiness. It will also provide key exercises and guidelines that other people have successfully followed to change their behavior and obtain true happiness.

Below are other key techniques you can use to make happiness happen for you.

- **Remember that when you get down at work, you create happiness by how you deal with what happens to you.** So when you feel that you are getting taken advantage of or when you feel that you are underpaid, think about how you are going to deal with these issues rather than stewing on them.

- **What you can't change, you can accept.** There is a lot at work to get upset about. Pick your battles. Let the small stuff go, and concentrate on the bigger things that will provide you more sustained happiness and fulfillment.

- **Be cautiously optimistic; don't just be blissfully ignorant**. Being optimistic and having a good attitude are absolutely important when achieving happiness at work. However, you can't be blind to "caution" lights that are blatantly obvious. Don't set yourself up for disappointment. If you throw your name in the hat for a promotion you are not qualified for and there are six other qualified candidates, don't be heartbroken when the opportunity does not pan out for you.

- **Always look for the good or the lesson learned in things that initially appear bad.** When you run into conflict, reflect back on what you have learned and how you can ensure it doesn't happen again.

HAPPINESS NOT HEREDITARY? NO PROBLEM!

Is your mother happy? Is she a pessimist or an optimist? In his book *Learned Optimism*, Martin E. P. Seligman explains that your mother and your teachers have the most influence on your "explanatory" style, on whether you see things as an optimist or pessimist. But he also explains that with cognitive therapy or concentrated behavior, it is possible to change your "explanatory" style to be more optimistic. If you can stop yourself every time you have a negative thought and spin the thought into something positive, you can actually train your mind to stop thinking negatively.

EXERCISE: WHAT'S YOUR HAPPINESS PERFORMANCE RATING?

In the book *Happiness* by Richard Layard, I learned that scientists can actually measure happiness. How would yours measure up if we took stock of it today? Here's one way to do it. First, ask yourself when you are the happiest. It could be when you are laughing at a joke your friend just told. Or it could be when you are curled up with a book in your favorite place. This situation will be your happiness level 10.

Every day for a week, write down what your average happiness level is.

	S	M	T	W	Th	F	S
Happiness Level Today							

In addition to measuring your average happiness level each day, it's important to reflect on reasons that your happiness level is not as high as you would like it to be. This will then enable you to address the issues either head-on that day, by recognizing them, or at the end of the week after reflecting on your week's results.

In the lines that follow, write down the reasons that your happiness level is not a 10. Strive to bring it up by 2 points each day. (If you find ways to make your happiness level go up, email me at bthomas@sequent.biz and tell me about them!)

Look for patterns. For example, maybe your happiness level is down on Sundays because your work week starts

HAPPINESS QUICK TIP

If you have someone hold you accountable to your goal, you will be much more successful at obtaining it. So try it. I want each of you to email a friend (or me!) your happiness rating now. Explain how you are going to increase your happiness and what strategies you will use. Keep in mind each one of us will have different strategies based on where we are now in our life and how we behave. Make sure you report on your progress at least two times a month.

the next day, or maybe your happiness level goes up on Thursdays as you get ready for the weekend.

REASONS I AM NOT HAPPIER TODAY

Sunday _____

_____

Monday _____

_____

Tuesday _____

_____

Wednesday _____

_____

Thursday _____

_____

Friday _____

_____

Saturday _____

_____

TAKING RESPONSIBILITY FOR YOUR TEAM'S ATTITUDES

When we talk about choosing happiness and owning attitudes, we're talking about an area where leaders truly need to lead.

One of the most common problems is having associates who are "stuck" in a negative attitude or resistant to change. Condoning this bad behavior makes you look like you approve of it and want it as part of your culture. You could be losing superstars if your company is infested by bad attitudes. It's up to you to not let one bad apple ruin the whole lot.

Unfortunately, leaders get caught up in "performance at all costs." What does this mean? It translates into leaders who are afraid of letting go of negative employees because they perform from a work perspective—even though these employees are large contributors to an uncomfortable workplace culture. These leaders (or should I say cowards?) support such employees rather than terminating them. Doing this hurts not only the overall culture of the business but the bottom line as well: even though you're perhaps gaining a little performance from one person, you lose performance from many others.

Specifically, I am talking about a person who may be perceived as a superstar from a work perspective, i.e., he or she moves the ball down the field day after day, works seventy to ninety hours a week, and holds a tough or executive position with the company. However, he or she is also a combative and difficult partner or employee, can't (or doesn't) build any relationships within the team, manages by threat and intimidation, and has the worst attitude around. These folks will help ruin your culture, and if you allow them to continue behaving this way, you share the blame for creating an ineffective, dysfunctional, and unhappy work environment.

I think of it this way: I don't care how smart you are, how

many advanced degrees you have, or even if you bring in more business than I can ever handle. If you can't get along with people, help others succeed for the greater good of the company, and be a team player, I have no place for you in my business.

The companies that do an exceptional job in weeding these people out perform well. The companies that fight a losing battle are the ones that have the reputation for a difficult work environment and that allow this environment to persist.

American Eagle Outfitters, for example, works hard at taking care of its people. The company is very protective of its caring culture. The employees who hurt that culture by behaving negatively are dealt with immediately.

Another example comes from my company, Sequent. When going through a downsizing last year, my CEO asked, "Who would you want on your island?" This was indicative of his attitude toward his top talent. It wasn't just those with great skill sets; it's those people you would want around when the going gets tough.

LEARNING MORE ABOUT HAPPINESS FROM THE PROS

Because different people find happiness in different ways, it can be helpful to review a variety of feedback from authors, scholars, and psychiatrists on what it means to be happy, how to find happiness, and how happiness can help you. As you read this list, think about how you relate to each statement, if you agree, or if something seems completely foreign to you. The more time you spend thinking about what happiness means, the easier it will be to find it for yourself.

- *The Last Self-Help Book You'll Ever Need: Repress Your Anger, Think Negatively, Be a Good Blamer, and Throttle Your Inner Child* by Paul Pearsall

  Wow, not sure if his message is the same as mine—perhaps we would be a good balance! Regardless, here are a few thoughts from his book that help elaborate the point of being realistic about your happiness.

  - Always thinking positively about tomorrow robs you of fully experiencing today.

  - "Mindful awareness" rather than positive thinking is the key to savoring life.

  - Just because self-help advice "sounds right" doesn't mean it is right. Maintain a healthy skepticism. Beware of your own biases.

  - Sometimes life is sad. Depression and grief are natural, not dysfunctional. Don't rush negative feelings.

- *The Happiness Hypothesis* by Jonathan Haidt

  This book discusses the genetic side of happiness, what heredity implies for happiness, and how important it is for your happiness. What do you think about the author's points?

- People are biologically wired for success but not necessarily for happiness.

- People may have a genetic "set point" for their level of happiness. You can change this set point through meditation, cognitive psychology, or medication.

- Though genetics accounts for a baseline level of happiness, other environmental and societal factors are influential. Some can be changed; others must be accepted.

- Humans are psychological, emotional, social, and spiritual. You must understand yourself in all these systems to understand what makes you happy.

- Doing what's easiest doesn't necessarily make you happy. Pursuing goals engages you in living.

- Progress in seeking happiness gives more pleasure than happiness itself.

In this chapter, you learned that you can choose how to deal with the events in your life.

As we see at work every day, crap happens. Whether it is fair or not fair, whether it is valid or not valid, you have a choice in how far you let it bring you down. That realization is empowering. You have the choice to overcome it, to create a strategy around it, and to make the situation different for yourself. This is a powerful place to be. It's a place where choosing happiness can bring you power—power over the unhappiness and power over the negativity that brings you down. If you realize that your work is not a place that you see ever being happy, it may be time that you create a new job strategy and start planning your exit to a new job, a new life, and a new level of happiness.

All of these hints, tips, and tricks will help you do more than just choose to be happy. They will help you to live happily.

:)

HAPPINESS TIP #3

AVOID WHAT HOLDS YOUR HAPPINESS HOSTAGE: MINIMIZING WORRY AND NEGATIVE THOUGHTS

In the small villages of Central America, rural craftswomen stitch together tiny sets of colorful figures they call worry dolls. As the folklore goes, you can share a worry with one of your dolls, place her under your pillow at night, and she'll do the worrying for you. When you wake up in the morning, your worry's gone! If this is a true story, I know a lot of people who must be housing a small army under their pillows at night.

HAPPINESS NOTE CARD: THE WISDOM OF WORRYING

There are a lot of world leaders, writers, artists, and business executives who have had plenty to worry about in their time. And a few have actually been quite reflective on the subject. The great Winston Churchill once said, "When I look back on all the worries, I remember the story of the old man who said on his deathbed that he had a lot of trouble in his life, most of which never happened." Entrepreneur Glenn Turner compared worrying to rocking in a rocking chair. "It gives you something to do, but it gets you nowhere," he said. Dale Carnegie, the well-known self-improvement expert, liked to ask, "Do you remember the things you were worrying about a year ago? Didn't you waste a lot of fruitless energy on account of most of them?" Even Jesus weighed in on the topic of worrying when he said, "Do not worry about tomorrow, for tomorrow will worry about itself. Each day has enough trouble of its own."

My own motto about worrying is pretty simple: "Keep things in perspective, and focus on the good."

Diane Dietz, Assistant Executive Director for the Ohio Health Care Association, states, "Worry at work causes insecurities that result in poor performance." She goes on to add, "Worry at work debilitates your creativity and uses up the time you need to get your job done right." With this in mind, understand that worrying not only robs you of your happiness, but also can hurt your career.

Training for a happier, more fulfilling experience at work means breaking down the barriers that stand in the way. This chapter explains how distorted thinking, replaying negative thoughts in your mind, and plain old worry can derail plans to be happier and more fulfilled. The tips in this chapter will help you reverse this thinking, lift yourself up instead, and create a positive outlook every day. You will learn how to deal with your negative thoughts and behaviors so that you can tackle your concerns in a productive, healthy way. You'll learn to take control of your worries (rather than letting them take control of you). You'll learn to identify what worries are taking up the most of your precious time, evaluate them, and finally learn how to make them disappear.

WORRY NATION

Worrying has become a national epidemic. It's a malady that affects our ability to discover, experience, and enjoy all the things that can make us really happy in life. The tremendous impact of worrying really hit home for me after I conducted an informal poll of dozens of friends and colleagues in preparation for this book. I couldn't believe how many of them said worrying was the number one thing that was holding them back from experiencing more happiness in their lives. They cited things like the following:

- "Worrying about the family finances"
- "Wondering if I'm doing the right things as a parent"
- "Worrying about performing on the job so I don't lose it"
- "Worrying that my career is at a dead end"
- "Getting stressed out watching every move my two teen-agers make"
- "Hoping I make my sales quotas every month—if I don't, it could mean the company loses jobs"

- "Worrying that I'll get cancer or some other big health problem"

- "What if I start to look awful as I age?"

This is the longest chapter in the book, and there's a big reason for that. Worry holds people hostage. I see corporate executives and individual contributors spend hours and sometimes days on worry. Overcoming and dealing with the worry that prevents them from performing or being happy at work is something for which people frequently request coaching.

It's not that hard to see why we worry so much: we're on information overload. With all the technology we're carrying in our pockets and purses, we have twenty-four-hour access to email messages (via our "CrackBerries"), our to-do lists, and plenty of news from around the world, most of which is bad. We feel intense competition to be better at work, better

ARE YOU WEARING YOUR WORRY?

Walk down a busy street or through a bustling shopping mall. Can you tell who's worried? Look at the facial expressions of those around you. When I did this exercise recently, I saw a lot of furrowed brows and downward stares. Are you one of those people? If so, then try this little pick-me-up. Keep your chin parallel to the floor. Hold your shoulders back and stand tall. And smile. Even if you've got worries on your mind, just changing your body language a little will help lift your spirits. Try it—it works.

in relationships, better as parents, and even better looking! High standards and lofty goals are great, but being performance- and results-minded has a downside: it puts even more pressure on us and creates more worries. The problem is, this huge investment we're making in our worries isn't paying us anything in dividends. Think about it. Would you put your money into something that paid you absolutely nothing in return? Heck no! So why invest so much of your time and emotion in something that does the same?

STARE IT DOWN: WHAT DO YOU WORRY ABOUT THE MOST?

I used to worry all the time. For almost twenty years, I sweated over whether I was making it on the job. I had deep-seated anxiety that I wasn't going to perform well enough to advance in my career, help my husband bring home the bacon, and most importantly, be able to keep my job. I worked diligently at my career. I did different kinds of work and got experience in several industries. I survived many different bosses—nice ones, mean ones, and stupid ones (and you know who you are out there!). Still, I spent the better part of two decades wondering and worrying: Am I making enough money? Am I smart enough? Does my boss hate me? Will I lose my job? How will my family be hurt if I do? I pulled on my boots every day and trudged off to work, carrying the weight of my worries with me.

Most of us have at least one "big kahuna" of a worry like this. You probably fret about a lot of little things throughout your day, but there's likely a giant-sized worry that's plagued you all your life. For me, it was this constant worry about my professional performance and wondering whether I would have enough money to pay for my kids' college and our retirement. For others, it's been a lifetime of worrying about money or about raising decent kids. One friend of mine has spent years worrying about being accepted by others.

How many times at work do you worry about not knowing something when asked or not performing up to the standards of your boss? I see people fret about a certain presentation or meeting for weeks before they have to do it. Every day closer to the "big" meeting or presentation, the look of worry only increases. One day I approached a colleague and asked him what he was so shaken up about. He explained he had his first meeting with his new boss (who replaced his old one). He'd worked for years to impress the old boss, and now he was about to make the first impression on the new boss. "Any advice?" he asked. I said, "Actually, yes. Why don't you prepare for it rather than worry about it? Create a list of the accomplishments you have achieved over the last several years, talk about your top priorities, and explain that you are passionate about your work and would love any feedback on how you can be a top performer in the organization."

I also love the question "If you were to say I did a *great* job six months from now, what would I have done?" This helps sets the stage of understanding what your boss values. Instead of spending all your time worrying, take control. Don't wear your worry; dress it up a bit and let it go.

It's time to look your worries straight on and stare 'em down. Why? Because they're sneaking into your life and stealing away what precious time you have to spend being blissfully and peacefully happy.

PUT YOUR WORRIES THROUGH A WORKOUT

So do you really know what's worrying you? What are the little things (and the "big kahuna") whittling away at your happiness every day? Well, there's an easy way to find out. Get some three-by-five-inch index cards, and every time a worry pops into your head, write it on a card. It can be simple notes, like "worrying I'm going to be late for this meeting," "worrying I'm not going to make this deadline," "worried I just made that store clerk mad," "worrying that Jessica is mad at me because I missed her birthday bash," or "concerned that my employee was crushed because I didn't like the presentation she worked on all weekend." For one whole day, don't miss a single worry. And you might want to get a flashlight so you don't forget to record the worries running through your head while you're in bed at night—those are just torturous!

Then, tomorrow, count up all your "worry cards." You may be surprised by all the things you fretted over in a single day. I bet if you had collected a separate set of cards to record all the things that made you happy in the same twenty-four-hour period, that pile would be much smaller. What would happen if you replaced that worry with happiness?

Let's look at how easy it is to work out some of those little worries you're carrying around with you every day. Just think how many of those worry dolls you'll be putting out of business! For starters, choose one of the worries you wrote down on a card. Now ask yourself four important questions:

1. What's the absolute worst that can happen?
2. Is that very likely to happen?
3. How can I handle this worry in a positive way?
4. Is there a way I can address it and fix it quickly?

Let's use the example of "worrying I'm going to be late for this meeting." Write down a few answers to the first question, such as, "I'll be fired on the spot"; "Someone will embarrass me by saying 'Nice of you to show up late' in front of the entire group"; "My boss will notice, and his view of me and my work ethic will diminish a bit." Now ask yourself, are those things really likely to happen? Maybe, but if so there are ways of dealing with it.

So how can you turn this worry into more constructive

and happier thinking? First, remind yourself that your worry might not come true. Sure, there's a lot of traffic, but maybe you won't be late. (Great job on that positive thought!) If you do arrive late, you'll have an opportunity to show others how you're able to handle an uncomfortable situation graciously. Not just anyone is capable of this. (Oooh, that's another good positive thought. You're on a roll!) Hey, when you do walk in late, everyone will notice the great outfit you're wearing today. (Now you're really thinking positive thoughts!) You'll be able to demonstrate accountability with your boss by admitting you made a mistake, apologizing, and promising it will never happen again. (Nice work on another positive thought!)

HAPPINESS QUICK TIP

Are you primed for a little inner peace? Sometimes the worst of our worrying kicks in when life gets chaotic and our stress levels go up. Try one of these things to momentarily bring your life back to a slower pace:

- Go to a yoga class or learn a simple meditation technique.
- Turn off the TV, your phone, and other electronics.
- Get out of the office and go for a drive.
- Listen to peaceful music.
- Dim the lights and fill the room with the smell of scented candles.
- Schedule a massage.
- Take a slow walk somewhere beautiful, and take in the blue sky, the breeze, and the sunshine.
- Vent your worry to a colleague or friend. Sometimes just saying it out loud makes you realize how silly it is.

Even better, there's a great chance you'll walk into that meeting a few minutes late and not a single person will notice. Think about all the worrying you would have done for nothing! I know this "power of positive thinking" is a bit cliché, but in this case, I believe it works. Turning what could be an insidious worry into constructive and positive thinking can bring a whole lot more tranquility and added happiness to your life.

CAN'T GET THAT THOUGHT OUT OF MY HEAD

When we take a microscope to our worries, we can see that they are driven by negative thoughts. When you think about something negative, your mind plays games with you. You let it become very creative and allow this negativity to play over and over in your head, perhaps until you aren't sleeping at night. How many times have you had a bad day at work, only to come home and find you couldn't sleep all? A client of mine told me a great strategy to combat this: write down your work challenges on a piece of paper next to your bed to free those worries from your head. You will find it helps you let go of your worries and catch some ZZZs the rest of the night.

Just as happiness is a choice, controlling these negative thoughts is also a choice. Let me be clear: negative thoughts (let's call them creepers, because they creep into our minds, mostly without warning) will probably always be a part of our lives; however, they don't have to control our lives. We can choose to deal with creepers the same way we deal with any of our business problems: we can analyze them and create a plan of action. When we deal with creepers as they come up rather than letting them fester to the point of taking control over our life, we will be much happier. Let's look at some of the ways we can do that.

SORTING OUR CREEPERS

Are all negative thoughts created equal? No way! There are two types of creepers, and understanding their differences can help us learn how to deal more effectively with them. Some creepers are based on real, factual evidence, such as a cancer diagnosis, company layoffs, or looming debt. Other creepers may feel just as real, but they aren't based on fact. These creepers appear when we let our imaginations run wild. We worry that a friend might be upset with us when she doesn't return a phone call, but perhaps we've just misinterpreted her busy schedule. Whether your negative thoughts are based on fact or fiction, you can gain control over them by developing a strategy to solve them.

The best way to handle creepers that are based on fact is to understand what you can and cannot control. This will go a long way toward making you feel better. Otherwise, your only option is to be paralyzed by fear and paranoia. Wouldn't you rather be happy and worry-free? That is certainly the best option, but it is your choice—and it does take work.

Need a few examples?

Let's say you lose your job. Sure, that is overwhelming and sad, but what are you doing about it? You shouldn't feel sorry for yourself (well, at least not for long) or spend time being mad at your former boss or company (well, again, not for long). Having a plan helps you take control of your worry and disables its ability to take control over you. Just creating the plan will make you feel better. And a positive attitude can help you overcome your fear. Let's look at an example of how one woman made a choice to overcome her worries.

One of my close friends—let's call her Lisa—lost her job. She was the breadwinner; her husband was a stay-at-home dad. They had just bought a new—and too expensive—home, and their two kids attended parochial schools. When I called to offer my condolences, Lisa said with a shrug in her voice, "Oh, well. That just means there is something better around the corner. I'll just make a better opportunity come along." Within twenty-four hours, not only did she have a "plan of attack," but she had also already started following through in a big way:

- Creating a list of companies to target

- Developing a "perfect-job scenario" of what she wanted

- Updating her résumé

- Joining LinkedIn (a professional social networking site)

- Signing up on executive search websites (6figures.com and execunet.com)

- Sending an email out to her friends to give them her new contact info and let them know that she was in search of a job

- Looking at alternatives, such as independent consulting, and creating an "offer sheet" for that possibility

Clearly she had the choice. Either allow a host of negative thoughts to enter her mind, curl up in the fetal position, and feel sorry for herself—or take control of the situation and make it better. At her level, job searches can take up to a year. However, with her careful planning and positive attitude, she had a job within six weeks—and it is a much better job that has made her happier than ever before. What a fantastic example of someone who is powered by happy. Tragedies can always turn into lucky charms. Turning a negative situation into a positive one can be one of the most enriching experiences you can have.

Another example of someone who chose to confront her creepers head-on is my best friend from first grade. She was diagnosed with Stage Two breast cancer at the young age of thirty-five. The doctor gave her six months to live. She could have immediately allowed negative thoughts to control her, to take over her illness and make her succumb, but she didn't. Against all odds, she beat the cancer for almost ten years, far longer than any doctor ever predicted. Her cancer never truly left her body; instead it spread just about everywhere, including to her pancreas and liver. Through her fight, she certainly had reason to get down or get negative, but she didn't allow those thoughts to control her. One time I had the courage to ask her if she was afraid of dying. She looked me square in the face and said, "I'm not going to die. Actually, I never even think about that." Instead of worrying about her fate or what her three young boys would do without a mother, she decided to take control and create a plan.

Her plan was as follows:

- Get the best medical care possible, seeking out second opinions from all over the country

- Become educated on treatment options—whether traditional or unconventional

- Demand the most progressive and proactive treatment possible, including getting scans every three months

- Live life to the fullest and stay preoccupied with the other great blessings she had in her life

- Maintain an incredible amount of faith and prayer and give her worry to God

- Keep the attitude that she would beat this horrible disease

There is no medical reason why my best friend survived so long. She fought this disease with every ounce of her body and soul. If she hadn't, she would have died years ago. But she didn't allow the creepers to take over. She didn't listen to statistics or any "normal" prognosis. Instead, she took charge of her destiny through positive thinking. This was the difference between six months and ten years. She concentrated on life rather than death. As a result of her positive attitude and dedication to following through with her plan, we enjoyed many wonderful and happy times during the last eight years—time most people would have spent consumed with negative thoughts.

We all have either been through these types of tragedies or know those who have. Sometimes they didn't have the faith or the attitude. Sometimes it was just too late. However, if you were facing a tragedy like this, would you want your last days, months, or even years to be filled with negative thoughts or with hope? This is where your attitude, your faith, and your plan come in. In situations like this, the way you deal with these negative thoughts can determine the quality of your life.

These negative thoughts are the basis for much of our worry. The difference between the two is that "worrying" happens after we allow those negative thoughts to take control of us, rather than us taking control of them. We need to control the negative thoughts as they come into our mind and train ourselves to stop them before we start to worry. It is cognitive behavioral training. When it comes into your mind, analyze it, deal with it, and move on.

EXERCISE: NEGATIVE NO MORE

When you're combating negative thoughts, it's interesting to take a look at which ones you tend to let in and why. Let's say you find yourself thinking a lot of jealous thoughts about your colleagues at work. Why? Is it because someone else was promoted and you were not? Did someone else get to lead the big project? Does it really get under your skin when someone offers public criticism of your work? Gaining insight about your most pervasive worries can help you identify what you must do to move forward.

Let's try breaking down some negative thoughts.

What negative thoughts do I have?

_____

_____

_____

_____

Are they real and based on facts? If so, what are those facts?

_____

_____

_____

_____

What actions can I take to deal with this issue head-on and overcome this worry?

_____

_____

_____

_____

WHEN IT'S ALL IN YOUR HEAD

Often the worry dolls we've stuffed under our pillows at night aren't based on bank accounts, layoffs, or frightening diagnoses. Instead, they're the products of our runaway imaginations. We start thinking about something and then imagine a terrible outcome, and before we know it, we've got a brand-new creeper! How many times have you spent valuable time worrying about something or someone without any real reason to do so? Perhaps you worried about whether your boss feels you add value or not, or about a relationship with a friend or family member that has gone south.

These dramatic, imaginary worries turn into negative stories we tell ourselves over and over again. Dealing with these thoughts directly and promptly is the best way to neutralize them. Every fictitious story takes up mental space you could be making for positive thoughts that would increase your happiness. When you start to create these stories, the best thing you can do is stop yourself, consider the facts, and determine if they are truly worth your time. This plan is much more effective when it is executed as soon as possible. The more you wait, the less freedom from worry you will have.

Here's an example of how my own negative imagination once got the better of me at work. Years ago, I was in a meeting when my boss ripped into me about a report I had created. It wasn't what he wanted, it didn't have the right information on it, and the format was all wrong. He made it very clear in front of all my colleagues that it did not meet his expectations. I left the meeting not just humiliated but also deflated and feeling like the definition of a "low performer." My mind automatically began to imagine a story. The story I told myself was that I was not performing as I should, that my boss (and colleagues) thought I was an idiot, and that my job was on the line.

After I left that terrible meeting, I redid that stupid report. I gave it to my boss and waited for his feedback. I waited and waited, and I heard nothing. Did he like it? Did he think it was still bad? Was my pink slip being drawn up?

Weeks went by, and I never got to "debrief" what happened in the meeting with my boss. He wasn't the warmest or most approachable boss I'd had; therefore, time passed, and things continued to feel cool between us. This, of course, made my imaginary story ten times worse. I had these negative thoughts for two more months, stewing over what my colleagues thought of me, what my boss thought of me, and how that one-hour meeting had triggered the demise of my career. I shared these thoughts and worries with not only my family but also my friends and other trusted colleagues. I was creating quite the story—and the story got more exaggerated every time I told it.

Finally, I couldn't take it anymore. I was paranoid, losing sleep, and not exactly fun to be around. My colleagues would start rolling their eyes every time I brought it up. I decided to take action, address it head-on, and schedule a meeting with my boss.

I started out by saying that I was really sorry that I did not meet his expectations on the report. I reassured him that it wouldn't happen again and that I would work harder to ensure I understood his expectations better to produce a result more in line with his needs. I paused and noticed that he was looking at me as if I had a second head. As he tilted his head to the side, he asked, "What report?" I carefully responded with every little detail from that dreaded one-hour meeting. He looked at me again, as if to say, "Holy crap! Are you kidding?" and quickly responded, "Oh my gosh, Beth, I totally forgot about that. The report you redid for me was exactly what I wanted. Sorry I didn't get back to you. I honestly meant to apologize weeks ago for the way I behaved in that meeting. I have been under a tremendous amount of stress lately, and taking it out on people like you, whom I value so much, was wrong. Please accept my apology."

What? Are you kidding? I had just spent two months of

my life having these negative thoughts consume me about my job, and he'd forgotten all about it? Did he know the stress I had been under? Did he know my family and friends were about ready to kick me to the curb if I talked about this one more time? Did he know the happiness he had robbed from me? Then I sat back and thought about it a bit more. He didn't rob me of anything. I had robbed myself. I chose to create a story and run with it. As bad and misinformed as it was, the story was mine, all mine. I took control, all right. But I did it in the wrong way. All those negative thoughts were based on imagination and not the truth, and I had wasted days, weeks, and months on something for no reason at all.

In the book *Crucial Conversations*, Kerry Patterson et al. explain the concept of "mastering your own stories," or learning to step back and deal with the facts, rather than filling in the blanks to create a story filled with imaginary details. When we force ourselves to look objectively at a negative scenario, we often find that the scariest parts of it aren't real at all. When we learn to "master our stories," we can save precious time and energy.

One day I was explaining to a friend just how much deep-seated anxiety I felt over performing well enough to advance in my career. He just smiled and said, "What are you so worried about? It's only work! At the end of the day, does work define who you are? Does that really drive your happiness? Has worrying about it ever, ever helped you do a better job?" Of course, the answers to his simple statements were resounding "nos." The more I thought about my friend's questions, the more they released me from the heavy burden of my worries.

I never again allowed my performance at work to be fueled by toxic worry. Being powered by happy meant that I would focus on my strengths and take every opportunity to learn new skills and contribute. I ensured that I always had a backup plan in the event that my job fell through. Instead of spending time worrying, I spent time networking in my industry so I would have contacts if I were job hunting. I volunteered for work projects that expanded the skills I could

HAPPINESS QUICK TIP

Want to have a great day that's filled with more happiness? Try this quick tip: promise yourself that for the next twenty-four hours, you won't utter a single negative statement or ponder a single negative thought. No complaining, absolutely no criticism. It might be harder than you think! But stomping out negative thinking can go a long way to helping you feel happier and more positive. Instead, replace negative thoughts with appreciation for all the things going right in your life.

put on a résumé. Oh, and guess what? I had a lot of fun doing these things! Plus, having a backup plan and a great network gave me a bit of security that helped eliminate my worry about job insecurity.

EXERCISE: NEGATIVE NO MORE, PART II

So, again, what are you thinking about today? Think about a worry you have right now, one that's based on a story you have created—one that's based only on fiction, not facts.

What is a story I have created in my mind right now that is causing me worry?

_____

_____

_____

_____

What are the fictitious elements of my story?

_____

_____

_____

_____

What are the facts?

_____

_____

_____

_____

What actions can I take to deal with this head-on and turn my nightmare into a happy ending?

_____

_____

_____

_____

BREAK YOUR ADDICTION TO WORRYING AND NEGATIVE THOUGHTS

Whether your creepers are based on things real or imagined, there are some overall strategies you can use to get any of these monkeys off your back.

It's actually easier than you might think. We just need to learn to reprogram the way our brains idle. Instead of allowing our brains to automatically fall into "worry mode," we need to intervene. The first step is to become aware of the topics your mind focuses on when you're not busy. Are you daydreaming? Or are you focusing on something negative?

Once you have developed the habit of checking in with your mind and noticing what you're focused on, you can learn to take the next step. While we can't stop our brains from thinking of worries, we can train our brains to ignore these worries. When you find yourself focusing on something scary or sad or unpleasant, stop! Think of a funny joke or something you're looking forward to.

If you babysit your brain this way, never letting it get into too much trouble, you'll find you're more aware of just how happy you've become.

HAND 'EM OVER TO A HIGHER POWER

As you've learned in this chapter, I absolutely believe you can take control of your worries and ensure they become less intrusive in your life. But the truth is, life does sometimes present us with situations where it's virtually impossible not to worry. You or a family member might be facing a serious illness. You may be having job or financial difficulties that are simply out of your control. I think of the parents, siblings, spouses, and kids who have said good-bye to loved ones as they were sent into military service. It's hard not to worry about them.

Years ago when a friend was going through a painful divorce, she found herself dealing with many challenges. She had to find a new place to live, and she felt concern about how her two boys would adjust. And there were lots of financial problems as the bills mounted up. Then the car broke down. Her self-esteem was at an all-time low. I asked her how she was coping with all the worries she faced. She simply said, "When it gets bad and I can't handle it any more, I just hand it over to God. I send it up to Him." I was struck by the simplicity and the wisdom of her statement. No matter what your religious beliefs, I believe we can all call upon a higher power to help us in times of deep and justifiable worry.

KEEPING THE WORRYING WORLD IN PERSPECTIVE

Finally, as you reflect on all those things you've struggled with and worried about lately, remember to keep things in perspective. It's easy to let the definition of "worries" get way out of kilter. I'm sometimes troubled when I see people worrying about whether they're driving the latest car, carrying the most expensive handbag, or being seen in the right places with the right people. Ours is a world filled with hunger, violence, poverty, and unspeakable tragedies. I actually feel guilty sometimes when I evaluate what I am worrying about. The things are sometimes minuscule compared to what others are going through. When you reflect on what has you so worried, think about what others have to worry about: losing a child, losing a job, going on welfare, being faced with a terminal illness. Then think again about what you were worrying about. If it is one of those minuscule things, put it in perspective and realize that life could be a lot worse. Why not feel simple gratitude for your good health, a steady job, a warm place to sleep at night, food on the table, and your friends and family around you? Start looking around and appreciating what you have, instead of worrying about what you don't. I guarantee you it will make your life happier and more meaningful in the end.

EXERCISE: HOW TO TRIM YOUR WORRY LIST

Since you're in training to eliminate some of the worries that are standing in the way of your happiness, let's do an exercise. Go back to that pile of worry cards you created earlier and let's officially put one into retirement.

Sort through your worry cards and select one for elimination. Rewrite it here.

_____

_____

_____

Now, on a scale of 1 to 10, with 1 representing "just not possible" and 10 representing "100 percent possible," rate your ability right now to eliminate this worry from your life.

_____

_____

_____

Now ask yourself these four questions about the worry topic you selected:

1. In the grand scheme of my life, is this issue really that big of a deal? Why? Say it out loud (so maybe you can hear how silly it sounds).

2. Am I actually making this worry worse for myself by focusing on it instead of on the things I need to do to address it? (Be honest.)

3. Are there a few simple things I could do to cope instead of mope about this worry? (I bet you can think of one or two right now.)

4. If things don't go the way I want them to, do I have the strength to put this worry in perspective and courageously deal with what comes next? (Of course you do!)

And now for the final part of this exercise: First, take a blank card and write three simple things you can do to fix or improve the issue you've identified. These should be things that will help you stop worrying and start feeling good about how you're addressing the challenge before you. Next, take that worry card we started with and shred it into tiny pieces. Make some confetti! Free it from your life forever!

Now look back at the "likely to eliminate" rating you assigned to this worry. With a little perspective, you should be closer to a 10. Sometimes just how to stand up to your worry releases you from it. Other times, knowing that you could deal with the worst-case scenario helps you cope and plan for a strategy or solution. Whatever your worry is today, don't let it hold you hostage. Focus on releasing its grip on you to gain back all those hours, days, and weeks you are wasting and that nobody deserves more than you.

WORRY HELP FROM THE EXPERTS

If these strategies did not offer you all the tips you need, the following page lists a few more from Dr. Timothy Sharp's Happiness Institute, with my commentary. These will help you deal with your negative thoughts more effectively.

- **Set aside a worry time.** Allow yourself to worry during this time slot, and then move on with your day.

- **Ask yourself, is the problem solvable?** If the problem isn't something you can solve, then move on to something you can control.

- **Be realistic.** Find solutions that are possible and within your reach.

- **Be aware of your negative thoughts.** Pay attention when they enter your mind. If you catch yourself blowing them out of proportion, stop! Then focus on helpful thoughts.

- **Be your best friend.** Encourage yourself and refocus your thoughts on positive things.

- **Use your heart as well as your head.** You can't always figure every problem out; sometimes you just need to deal with what is.

- **Keep calm.** You can't help yourself if you can't focus on what is happening.

- **Be mindful.** Worries often center on the future. When you focus on the present, you'll be unable to spend as much time focused on your worries.

- **Don't forget to sleep.** Lack of sleep only makes your worry more intense. It's difficult to think clearly enough to take control of your worry and move on.

• **Don't think you have to do it all on your own.** Rely on your support network for help and fresh perspective.

Today I freed myself from several negative thoughts that had weighed on my heart, and I am so much happier. I was worrying about a relationship with a dear friend of mine who moved away with her family. I took her move very personally, and I was hurt and angry that she would want to leave me for a better life. It took me six months to realize how terribly selfish that was. I spent days, weeks, and even months worrying about how we got to this point, whether we would ever be friends again, wondering what I should do. Well, I figured it out. By writing this chapter, I was inspired to create a plan of action. My plan was to recognize why we were both hurt, ask for forgiveness, ask to bury the hatchet, move on, and figure out how we could be as close with a long-distance friendship. I encourage and challenge you to set yourself free from a worry that has had control over your mind and happiness, as I did today.

The bottom line is that we are wired to have negative thoughts. Some are valid; some are not. Some are factual; some are fictional. It is up to us which scenario we allow to happen more often and which thoughts we allow to spiral out of control. What we need to do to increase our happiness is control the thoughts coming into our mind, analyze them quickly, and either deal with the negative ones or discard them.

Those negative thoughts are stealing time from your positive thoughts and utmost happiness. The more you allow those negative thoughts to come into your mind, the more you are training yourself to continue to think negatively.

The challenge I have for you is to stop. Start small. Every day, try to diminish the time you spend on worrying. Reflect at the end of each day on how much time you spent worrying. Hold yourself accountable to making that time diminish to the point that your new habit is replacing your worry with positive thoughts.

HAPPINESS P.S.

Giving up life as a chronic worrier could actually have health benefits. Do a quick search online, and you'll find dozens of studies that clearly show how stress and anxiety are connected to illness and disease. That's why it's a great idea to add "worry less" to your regular workout routine!

HANG WITH A GANG THAT GETS IT

Back when many baby boomers were wearing bell-bottom jeans and tie-dyed T-shirts, keeping a positive attitude was so important to the culture of the cool, hip, and happening set that any negativity at all was challenged with a retort that went something like, "Whoa, man, don't bring me down." While the hippie and dropout culture got a lot of things wrong back in the Dark Ages, perhaps this is one principle that has stood the test of time.

HAPPINESS NOTE CARD: A HAPPY ATTITUDE MAKES ALL THE DIFFERENCE—TO OTHERS

Having a good attitude creates a positive impression, no matter what your age. At a recent party I attended, a ten-year-old girl instigated a fight with the other children at the dinner table because no one wanted to sit by her. Why? Because, as I found out later, the other kids didn't think she was much fun to be around. This otherwise normal and even pretty girl never smiled. Her dour attitude was so obvious that my husband leaned over to me and said, "Do you think it would kill her to smile?" Maybe you know an adult who reminds you of a grown-up version of this little girl. Do you want to get stuck with that person at a party?

In this chapter, you'll learn the importance of surrounding yourself with positive people. You'll learn to evaluate your gang and consider how it affects your happiness.

YOUR GANG CAN DRAG YOU DOWN OR LIFT YOU UP

Remember that your happiness isn't just affected by your own state of mind. It can be greatly affected by your environment and the people in it. And that's something you can control. As the bell-bottom generation once preached, negativity brings everyone down. Have you ever noticed that when someone goes on and on about a difficult boss, a stressful day with the kids, an opposing political view, or even the crummy weather, you start feeling drained of energy?

I once worked with a person who seemed happy on the outside but was miserable on the inside. And she spread this misery in very manipulative ways. She would charm her way into an "inner circle" of folks and then talk behind their backs, trying to get ahead. This became toxic to her relationship with me as well as with everyone else she became "friends" with. It ultimately began to affect the culture in the organization.

Do you have people around you who are like this? No matter what you do or how positive you are, these folks will find a way to bring you down, even if they don't mean to. Does this make you want to spend time with them? And are these the kind of people who will ultimately help you achieve your goal of living a happier life?

Compare how those people make you feel with how you feel in the company of people who are upbeat and optimistic. You know the ones I'm talking about. They smile. There's a twinkle in their eye. Their body language communicates a certain openness. And as the old saying goes, they seem to be able to find the silver lining in every dark cloud. A few minutes in their company and you feel better almost immediately. That's because positive people create positive energy for those around them. It's contagious! Negativity simply isn't an option.

My friend Julie and I often laugh about the time I called her from work to set up a lunch date. I was distracted and multitasking, as usual. When her voicemail recording ended and it was time to leave my message at the tone, my brain went completely blank. I simply could not remember whom I had called. All that came to mind was to begin sweetly singing, "Oh fa la la la la, fa la la la la." I figured, "Hey, it was a more positive thing to do than hang up or swear into her answering machine out of frustration!" That was almost ten years ago. To this day, Julie and I still affectionately call each other "Fa La La." When she calls to chat, she'll sing, "fa la la" into my voicemail in different notes—some deep, some high, some sour. It never fails to give me a good belly laugh. Julie and I spend most of our time together laughing, and it can lift a dark cloud from any day. Just the other day, she sent me a note with a special quote about the importance of laughter. Her note read, "Dear Fa La La, It's no wonder that I always feel so good with you! Thanks for all the laughter!" Here's the quote she included:

"People who laugh actually live longer than those who don't laugh. Few persons realize that health actually varies according to the amount of laughter."

—James J. Walsh

Julie is definitely one member of my gang who really gets it. She's made a great contribution to my happiness over the years because of the positive attitude she possesses and the one she always inspires in me.

It's important to seek out this type of gang member at work. When I worked at the Limited Brands, 90 percent of the associates there were extroverts, fun, outgoing, and ready for a good time (we had a lot in common). When I went to Bank One, it was the opposite. About 10 percent of the associates had that extrovert personality I could connect with. I looked hard and long to find that 10 percent to hang with and eventually found an amazing group of individuals that made my time there all the better (Ellen, Steve, Paul, Don, and Andy). If it were not for these wonderful gang members, my time there would have been much more difficult.

Just as we tell our kids, you are guilty by association. If you hang with a negative gang, people who don't know you will assume you are just like the gang. This happens in corporate America all the time. I have seen innocent associates categorized in a bad way because of the gang they associate with. The last thing you want to do is get lumped in with the nag of the office or the "biotch" of the office or the Teflon man of the office (nothing sticks to me!).

Hang around the superstars instead—people who are positive, encouraging, and motivating. My father, Jack. R. Comas, had a motto: "Big people talk about success and ideas; little people talk about other people." I have tried hard to live by my father's words. They help me evaluate the types of people I want to associate with. Not only are the superstars fun, not only do they have a great attitude, but they may also help you become more successful. As I've said before, happy associates are productive associates. These are the ones that are seen as the up-and-comers, and, by association, you'll be seen this way, too.

EXERCISE: EVALUATE YOUR GANG

So here are some important questions: Who's surrounding you, and what effect are they having on your happiness? Do they really get it? Is the gang you're hangin' with (and I'm talking about your friends, family members, co-workers, neighbors, fellow volunteers, classmates, employees, and acquaintances) adding to your happiness or subtracting from it? It's time to do the math!

Now, I know what you're probably thinking. You're wondering, "How on earth is it possible to surround myself with only positive people?" After all, you don't really have control over the choice of your boss. You just happened to give birth to a naturally cranky kid. Your grouchy grandpa is a built-in part of the family. I get it! But remember that you do have significant control over the majority of the people with whom you spend your time. Being choosier about putting positive people around you can make a big difference, especially at work.

So now's the time to take an inventory of the people with whom you spend most of your waking hours. Write their names here:

_____

_____

_____

_____

_____

_____

_____

_____

_____

As you look at the list, note the effect each person has on your mood and frame of mind. Ask yourself these questions about each member of your gang:

Does he or she

• have a good professional reputation?

• have a successful career?

• build good relationships at work?

• have a positive tone of voice when you talk in person and by phone?

• have at least one upbeat and positive thing to say during your conversations?

• make you laugh?

• find something positive in negative situations?

• offer occasional compliments, encourage your feelings, and lift your spirits?

Or does he or she

• always have an issue with the boss?

• always feel treated unfairly at work?

- never make enough money?

- sound whiney and use negative words like "I'm not" or "I can't"?

- complain about everything and constantly sound exhausted or weary?

- always take the opposing view and find something negative in every situation?

- dismiss any positive things you have to offer?

- make you feel worse than when you began the interaction?

If you're checking off many of the things on the second list, it may be time to take a second look at those relationships. For sure, no one can be upbeat and positive all the time. That's not realistic. But if you're hanging around people who are chronically crabby, think about how that's affecting your happiness for the moment, for the day, and even for your lifetime.

You've categorized each of the primary people in your life as positive or negative. Now it's time to evaluate how they're affecting you. Next to each name, write down how much time you currently spend with him or her, then how much time you'd like to spend. How does each person impact your happiness? This activity can help you evaluate your most important relationships and whether they're helping you meet your lifelong happiness goals.

Friend	Positive?	Time spent together?	Time we should spend together?	Impact on my happiness?	Successful?	Negative?
Dan	No	6 hours a week	1 hour a week	Bad impact	Nope	Yep
Ellen	Yes	1 hour a week	4 hours a week	Increases	Yes	No

If doing this exercise has shown you that you're spending time with a negative person, it may be time to either break up or change the nature of the relationship. Breaking up is hard to do—yes, it is. I've come to learn that breakups aren't just for romantic relationships. Many times a breakup deals with a friend or family member, and that isn't easy either.

I had a friend whose relationship with her family (mostly her parents) was so toxic that she spent many days and nights in tears over their relationship. As much as she tried, as much as she went to counseling, nothing seemed to warm up this very chilly relationship. But it was her family! How could they not love her? How could they deny their own grandkids? How could they turn their back on their relationship with their daughter? It was starting to not only ruin her own life but also become the topic of discussion with her husband and friends every day. It was overwhelming. She was physically ill from worry and sadness. She tried calling, writing emails, even traveling two hours to pay them a visit. Her own parents turned her away.

One day she realized that she couldn't continue living

this way; she couldn't continue with this relationship. It was time to bury the fantasy of having a fairy-tale family life with her parents. The dream was over; the nightmare was over. It was time to move on. And boy, did she move on. She moved across the country for a new life with her own family and never looked back. The breakup had to happen for her to enjoy life again. Was it hard? Absolutely! But it was much harder living a life of sadness with those people around who robbed her of her happiness every day.

Recently Keri Dietz, an Allstate Insurance executive, explained to me how impactful hanging around positive, successful people has been for her career. She stated that when she was just starting out in the working world, she clung to a group of people who were constantly complaining about work and did everything they could to get out of work. She didn't know any different because she hadn't had time to get to know who was who around the office. She would stop by the desks of these folks only to find them shopping online or gossiping about harmless employees. They were the first to complain about the company or their boss at lunch. However, one evening she was out with friends and ran into an executive from the office.

As they all had a few drinks, the executive said to her, "The gang you are hanging with is bad news. I understand you didn't know any better when coming in to the company, but you may want to separate yourself from them. They are not on a good path here and I don't want to see the same thing happen to you."

Keri had no idea executives were noticing who she was associating with, but she appreciated the warning before her friends started to impede her own success at Allstate. Keri politically navigated herself away from that group and found herself seeking out those who appeared well liked, happy, and successful. Within months of finding new friends, Keri's career seemed to take off. She thrived in the midst of success. She thrived in the midst of happiness. She thrived with her group of friends talking about success and ideas rather than other people. This ignited Keri's attitude toward work: she truly felt she was powered by happy.

BUT I CAN'T FIRE MY BOSS!

Of course, I recognize you can't always just "fire" or navigate away from someone who may not be the most positive person in the world. We unfortunately don't have a choice with everyone at our work. Sometimes you just have to make lemonade out of lemons. There will most likely always be people at work who are not your type or people who are not good for you to hang with. For the most part, you can limit your time with these folks, keep a professional distance from them, and focus on your work and the gang you want to be associated with.

Sometimes, however, you find that you are an anomaly, and the culture doesn't support the type of people you most love to hang with. Sometimes it's not the right company or culture for you to be a part of. And if you're truly committed to living a happier life, you must start putting yourself in the company of more and more positive people.

SEEK OUT POSITIVE PEOPLE: CREATE A PERSONAL BOARD OF DIRECTORS

Some years ago, I came up with a way to make sure I was surrounding myself with people who supported my goals and made me feel great about my life plans. In essence, they would become my happiness coaches.

I call them my "personal board of directors." They're childhood friends, old neighbors, trusted family members, former bosses, professional colleagues, and even past clients. They're people whose opinions I respect and whose own personal behavior, integrity, and beliefs I admire.

Who would these folks be in your life? Take some time to consider who should be on your personal board of directors. Once you've thought about who would be best, ask them! Talk to them about how and when you'll solicit their advice and personal feedback. Assure them that their candid conversations with you won't cause any conflict with your relationship, even when it involves things you won't especially want to hear. Personal growth only occurs when the people you respect most are able to tell you the good, the bad, and the ugly about yourself. It's a good idea to meet with them every few months or once a quarter to keep you on track.

Here's an example of how to ask someone to be on your personal board of directors:

Felicia, I am working on my personal development as a leader. With that in mind, I am forming my own personal board of directors to seek feedback in regards to my performance or the struggles I may come up against. Since I respect your position as an executive, I believe I would gain much from your perspective and advice, and the lessons you've learned throughout your career.

Here are some of the questions you can pose to your personal board of directors:

- What do you see as my passions?
- Am I in the right career?
- What can I do to enhance my career and be happier in the work I do?
- From what you know about me, what changes do you think I should consider that would help me live a happier life?
- Do you see any obstacles I'm placing in the way of my happiness?
- What are the most inspiring things you're doing in your life to make you happy?

- How do you think others perceive me? Do you see any personal improvements I could work on?

- Can you give me advice or help me solve a problem that's causing some unhappiness in my life right now?

I guarantee you'll walk away from "board meetings" feeling more satisfied and energized than ever. You'll learn, as I have, that human beings can transfer their happiness to others in a positive way. Hanging with a great personal board of directors will give you that experience. So start electing your members now!

FEEDING BACK

Another great activity to do with your personal board of directors—or any of your acquaintances, for that matter—is to exchange positive feedback. This is something that rarely occurs with your co-workers, let alone your friends, but it's extremely valuable. Tell your directors or acquaintances that you would like to let them know how they have positively impacted your life. Then ask them to do the same. You can do this in writing, over lunch, or over the phone—but do it. You'll be surprised at how good it makes everyone feel.

If you are brave enough, I would challenge you to do this at work. Pick some of your most trusted colleagues, and find out what you have done at work that has positively impacted them and vice versa. You are not only learning what you can continue doing but also identifying which of your traits is most valued by others. It is a self-reflection that is validated by those working closest with you. It helps you understand how to build those interpersonal relationships that are critical to workplace happiness.

EXERCISE: GROOMING YOUR GANG TO BE HAPPY

This exercise can be an effective way of building team rapport, for a team you either manage or consult with. Gather the group together in a circle and put someone in the middle in the "hot seat." Have each person in the circle say one thing he or she appreciates most about the person in the hot seat. This helps instill a positive work environment among team members, helps build their self-esteem, and helps make them happy, all of which translates to increased productivity and better results. Rotate everyone into the hot seat to spread the happy.

Here's another exercise to celebrate a work effort that just ended successfully. Recognize specifically what each employee did well, and let each employee talk openly about the contributions the team made and how much it was appreciated. This not only makes everyone feel like the hard work was rewarded, but it also helps to instill camaraderie among the team members.

A friend of mine makes a habit of taking note of the things she is grateful for at the end of each day. She calls her habit "naming her highs." If her friends do something that makes it into her "high" category, the next day she lets them know. At first people don't know what to say when she calls them up saying, "Just wanted to thank you for one of my 'highs' yesterday. That joke you told was so funny!" But by doing this, my friend is acknowledging that the actions of her friends are important and, most of all, appreciated. Because she is so open about expressing her gratitude for those around her, many of her friends have picked up the habit.

Another friend of mine has started a wonderful birthday tradition among her group of friends. Whenever any of them has a birthday dinner, she asks everyone to come prepared with a note of gratitude for the guest of honor. People can either read their note aloud or just give it as part of their gift. The notes of gratitude range from short notes thanking a friend for her sense of humor to long stories about how she offered support in a time of need. Whatever the contents of the note, the message is the same: thank you for being a wonderful friend. What a way to celebrate a friend's birthday. I've seen more than one birthday girl burst into grateful tears after hearing the wonderful things her friends have told her.

You don't have to start a grand tradition or a quirky habit to offer positive feedback to your friends or colleagues. You can start small. Here are a few suggestions for starting to exchange feedback with your acquaintances:

• Give compliments to a manager about something he or she did well.

- Compliment colleagues or business associates on what they do well.

- Thank people that have been mentors or coaches to you and tell them specifically how they have helped you in your career.

- Invite a few friends to a "gratitude brunch," and ask each person to tell one thing he or she is grateful for.

- Write postcards to several of your friends, telling them you appreciate them.

- Call a family member and thank him or her for being a positive influence in your life.

- Send text messages to friends, telling them how much you enjoy their company.

- Give a friend a "gratitude journal," and write on the first page how much you appreciate him or her.

SWEET OR SOUR: EXACTLY HOW ARE YOU PERCEIVED BY OTHERS?

Up to this point, we've talked about associating yourself with people whose positive attitudes can have an affirming influence on your life. But what about the effect you're having on those very same people? We've talked briefly about this in "Feeding Back," but that focused on hearing the positive things. It's time to look a little more objectively at how your own attitude and everyday demeanor are affecting the important people in your life. Are you the one dragging everyone else down?

If there's one important goal I hope to achieve with my life, it's to make a lot of people around me happy. But, hey, perception is everything. Sometimes we simply can't see ourselves the way others do. Thinking of this, I decided that in preparation for writing this book, I should assess how others view me. I wondered, am I as positive as I think I am, or am I really a curmudgeon living in a dream world? That's when I decided to ask some of the people closest to me two simple questions. Here's what I found.

QUESTION #1: WHEN YOU THINK BACK ON THE TIMES WE'VE SPENT TOGETHER, HOW DOES IT MAKE YOU FEEL?

- "I smile because you always make me laugh and you're so funny."—My daughter Tiffany

- "The word that comes to mind is *happy*."—My best friend from grade school

- "Motivated and very upbeat."—One of my managers at work

- "Like we can achieve anything together."—My boss

- "You are so much fun! I love that we always laugh and joke."—My assistant at work

- "I think of the people I've introduced you to who instantly loved you."—A former co-worker

- "Whoa—better give me a specific timeframe you're referring to."—My husband

Try this exercise with those close to you and see if your results are a surprise!

QUESTION #2: ON A SCALE OF 1–10 (10 BEING THE MOST POSITIVE), HOW POSITIVE A PERSON DO YOU THINK I AM?

- "10"—My daughter Tiffany

- "10"—My best friend from grade school

- "12"—One of my managers at work

- "10"—My boss

- "10"—My friends Gina and Suzanne

- "Off the charts!"—A former co-worker

- "How positive you are would depend on whether or not I have emptied the dishwasher that day."—My husband

My husband's kidding aside, I was thrilled with this report. I've always worked at being a positive and happy person (thus, the reason for this book!), but here it was, validated by some of the most important people around me.

So what is reality for you? Do people want to hang with

you? Do they give you lame excuses when you ask them to get together? Do they return your phone calls? Maybe it's time to get in tune with the attitude you're projecting and how others really see you. I'm always amazed how many people believe they are perceived by others. Sometimes they have no clue! Without knowing it, your own attitude could be contributing to the unhappiness of others. In many companies today, it's not uncommon for managers to be required to solicit feedback from their bosses, their peers, and their employees so it can be included in performance reviews. For many of the colleagues I've worked with over the years, this often anonymous feedback has been absolutely devastating. They had no idea that people around them viewed them as disrespectful, unapproachable, arrogant, unmotivating, or even hostile.

But therein lies an opportunity. What a wonderful chance to change how you impact the lives of those closest to you. Asking your colleagues, friends, and family members how they perceive your attitude is a worthwhile investment of your time. Why? Because it means you're on your way to being part of other people's "happy gang." It's the gift that keeps on giving both to them and to you.

MANAGING HAPPINESS

My friend Michael is a senior sales executive for a company that started small in the Midwest and was later acquired by a Wall Street firm. As often happens in acquisitions, roles changed and many folks were terminated. Michael was happy to have survived the turmoil, but he found himself with a smaller job, a smaller office, and a lot less executive prestige. He knew his Ivy League–educated bosses on Wall Street saw him as a bit of a country bumpkin. They assigned him to the toughest industries and clients and gave him some of the biggest, most unattainable sales goals. Often on national conference calls, when it was his turn to report the week's accomplishments, his boss would quickly dismiss him. But as a manager, he was undeterred. He focused on his team. They often felt dejected, like they were being asked to perform against all odds. Michael knew that even with cuts in sales commissions and territories, he still had a great deal of control over the happiness of his team. Every week, he told them, "I will do whatever I can to help make you better." When times got tough, he said, "I will give you the skills that will make you the best candidate for jobs elsewhere, if need be." He rehearsed them for presentations and honed their sales skills. He recognized their accomplishments regularly and showed an interest in their personal lives and challenges. Their happiness and satisfaction was important to him.

Their results soared. His team soon was taking on additional responsibility and more clients, and Michael gained the respect of management. While the culture in Michael's organization remains very tough, he accomplished many things by managing the happiness of his team. The financial results naturally followed.

When I worked for the Limited Brands, I was responsible for all Y2K training. This involved training all seven companies within the Limited Brands on all new systems and processes. At first I thought I was being set up to fail. It was an overwhelming challenge. However, I looked at it as an opportunity and worked very hard over a two-year period. The people who worked for me throughout this process were also extremely committed to our goal, but I never let myself lose sight of their happiness. I was constantly checking in with them to ensure they were okay with their workloads and giving them comp time every minute I could. We also had a ton of fun. It was a project in which we all worked hard but did it as a team, and that kept the culture light and productive. In the end, it turned out to be an experience of a lifetime for all of us—and one that resulted in many promotions.

I will never forget when the project was all finished and the accolades and notes of thanks started to pour in from the top. When sharing this recognition with my team members and thanking them for their commitment to their work, one associate looked at me and said, "I would walk over hot coals for you." I knew then that my commitment to my team and the respect I'd showed them at all times had paid off.

Because they knew how much I valued them, they valued me in return.

HAPPY ASSOCIATES ARE PRODUCTIVE ASSOCIATES

An entire team powered by happiness—not by poor morale, stress, or negativity—has the potential to overcome many obstacles and outperform even its biggest competitors. I travel frequently, and my favorite airline to fly is Southwest. This company faced the same terrible downturn everyone else in their industry experienced following the September 11, 2001, terrorist attacks. It endured the same challenges of rising fuel costs, bad weather, and maintenance problems. But every time I board a Southwest flight, its employees seem genuinely happy to see me. It doesn't come from a script; it seems to come from inside the entire organization. Even on the toughest travel days, Southwest employees' upbeat attitudes—from the pilot and the flight attendants to the ground crew members—can always take the edge off a lot of crabby, unhappy passengers.

Southwest is legendary for its focus on hiring and developing happy employees, and I think it shows in its results. The company has been consistently profitable and is almost always top ranked in passenger satisfaction. It must be a great place to work when you're surrounded by two significant accomplishments: a lot of happy employees and a tremendous financial performance to be proud of.

The companies that win are companies in which the CEO is visible to the associates and concerned about the culture they work in. I have seen many good cultures throughout my consulting years as well as many bad cultures. One example of a CEO who really gets it is Jim O'Donnell from American Eagle Outfitters. The culture that Jim and his associates have built feels very entrepreneurial: each associate is valued independently and has a voice when creating the vision and strategy of the company. Fun is also part of the company's values and mission. When walking around corporate headquarters, you can actually feel how happy and engaged everyone is. And this attitude has translated to a very successful company. Associates actually feel valued and enjoy the work they do.

Michael Rempell, COO of the NYC design operations for American Eagle, is constantly concerned about the happiness of his associates, and it has paid off. They all love to work for him and are loyal to him because of it. It's the same situation with the chief supply chain officer, Joe Kerin. He is always seeking ways to recognize and reward his star associates. This is a huge motivating factor. It seems that everywhere you go in the American Eagle offices, you're running into one dynamic manager after another.

It's not only the attitude of the leaders who are driving this company but also the activities they do to help associates feel valued and recognized for hard work—things like picnics in the summertime and half-day Fridays from Memorial Day to Labor Day. These leadership styles and company perks make the employees want to "hang" at work. Employees look forward to coming to work every day and doing everything they can to protect their positive corporate culture.

Does your office feel happy? Can you make it feel happier?

HAPPINESS P.S.

Sometimes the greatest wisdom is the kind that's been around for a while. Long before I was born, a great book was published on the very power of positive people I've talked about in this chapter. Try reading the 1950s classic *The Power of Positive Thinking* by Norman Vincent Peale. It offers some great advice on the topic of happiness. My favorite chapter is "A Peaceful Mind Generates Power."

:)

DUMP THE TO-DO LIST AND START AN I-WISH LIST

Remember the endearing Disney song "When You Wish Upon a Star"? There's a lot of good advice in the lyrics of that little tune. The most memorable part, of course, is that when you perform the title action, it "makes no difference who you are, anything your heart desires will come to you." It was written in the late 1930s by a Pennsylvanian named Ned Washington, a man who preferred poetry to music and who must have understood the power of dreams. Making wishes might seem terribly frivolous and unrealistic to a lot of people, but I believe it's an important secret to the pursuit of happiness. That's why I recommend that everyone keep a wish list, not just a daily to-do list.

HAPPINESS NOTE CARD: THE REFUSE-TO-DO LIST

A friend of mine has a great strategy for when she gets overwhelmed by a lengthy to-do list that's getting in the way of her happiness. She stops and makes a refuse-to-do list. She jots down a brief list of things she knows she simply must stop doing in order to regain some control over her hectic life—things like "stop trying to find the perfect gift for the baby shower" or "stop gossiping about how horrible my boss really is." Refusing to answer the phone as often or deciding not to listen to bad news stories on TV may also be things that show up on the list. This is a great way to reduce your stress and reclaim the happiness you're entitled to feel. Sometimes it's not about what you do but what you simply don't do.

I can hear you saying now that "refuse-to-do" is impossible at work. Of course, you can't refuse to do work if you want to keep your job. However, you can refuse to do things that cause you harm at work. For example, you can refuse to get caught up in gossip, refuse to talk negatively about your colleagues, and refuse to cop an attitude when things don't go your way.

In this chapter, you'll learn how wishing can help you find greater happiness. But it's not as simple as just wishing on a star and then sitting back and waiting for it to come true. You'll learn to articulate your wishes and then develop a plan of action to help you achieve each and every one.

MAKING THE SHIFT FROM TO-DO LISTS TO WISH LISTS

There's no question that we live in a list-obsessed society. Every author wants to land a spot on the bestseller list.

Celebrities want to be on the "it" list and the best-dressed list. There are even books about lists! But in our fast-paced, time-managed world, it's pretty tough for many of us to live without our ubiquitous to-do lists. They tell us what we've got to do and where we've got to go.

I admit I'm as guilty as anyone. I cross one thing off my list and add another. I'm cranking out a fresh to-do list just about every twenty-four hours. Whew! One day, though, I sat down and looked at my list-making habit with fresh eyes. What was I really accomplishing? The answer was a lot of chores! I was getting the laundry done, getting the groceries and the school supplies purchased, getting my budget reports turned in at work, even getting my taxes finished. Checking these things off my list made me feel good—but only in the moment. I recognized that none of the items on the lists I was crafting day in and day out were making me feel truly fulfilled.

Beatle John Lennon wrote a great verse in a song he composed for his young son years ago: "Life is what happens while you're busy making other plans." I wondered if I was so busy making plans to get stuff done that I wasn't really doing what I loved. To look at it another way: was I so focused on getting things done that I wasn't focused on doing fun things I wanted to do for myself? Neglecting the fun would surely have an impact on my happiness at work.

I decided to change my thinking. From that point on, I pledged to keep two lists: one with to-dos and one with to-wish-fors. I took out a journal and wrote well into the night. I wished for a more fulfilling career with a boss who supported my goals instead of one who made me feel like a failure. I wished for a place where my family and I could retreat on weekends and holidays and to spend quality time together. I wished for a closer connection to God, not for one that was merely convenient. I wished for the wisdom and energy to write a book so I could share my beliefs about happiness with others. And, yes, I wished to lose ten pounds!

As I mulled over my wish list and that old to-do list, the difference between them really jumped off the page. My to-do list was an inventory of things that gave me a short-term sense of accomplishment and kept my daily life in order. And my to-do list changed almost daily. My wish list, on the other hand, was composed of things I believed would bring me enduring happiness over the long term, and it remained the

---

HAPPINESS QUICK TIP

Here's a fun and novel way to bring your wish list to life: visualize it! Buy a piece of poster board at your local craft store. Gather up catalogs, magazines, photos, greeting cards, or postcards. Collect your favorite poems and words of inspiration. Spend some quiet time clipping words and images that represent the things on your personal wish list. With your scissors and glue, create a colorful collage you can keep somewhere in your home that will always remind you of the happiness you're striving for. Want even more fun? Have a "Wish Upon a Star" party and do it with your friends.

same for a long time, which would ultimately affect my happiness at work, too.

MAKING A WISH LIST THAT WORKS

Over the years as I've created my own wish lists and encouraged others to do the same, I've learned a lot about the process. First, I've recognized that it's not easy. Come holiday gift-giving time, I've certainly never had a problem creating a "shopping wish list" for my husband. My wish list of colleges I hope my daughters will consider was easy to write. And I don't get stumped coming up with wishes for how I'd love to redecorate and improve our home. But wishes for enduring happiness at home and at work are a different story. They take a lot of contemplation and examination of where I am in my career and my life overall. They require a clear head and a willingness to think about what really matters in life. They beg some big questions that include, "Why am I here on earth?" and "What was I brought here to do?"

As you prepare to create your own wish list, here are a few things that might help guide you.

GUIDELINE #1: MAKE WISHES THAT REALLY CAN COME TRUE

Sometimes when people hear me talk about this idea of a wish list, they're skeptical. Someone once said to me, "Beth, surely you aren't suggesting people just sit around wishing for things to happen." Of course, the simple act of creating a list won't make your wishes come true. You must still take the right steps and do the hard work to bring them to life. From time to time, you may even have to adjust your expectations.

When I think about some of the wishes I've made over my lifetime, some came true, some are still within my reach, and some I simply had to let go of. Some are even wishes that developed in hindsight, when the opportunity to change things was long gone. From time to time, I've even had to give myself a wish-list reality check. For example, I've spent a lot of time wishing I'd gone to a college out of state and joined a sorority, rather than attending classes at the local college and living at home. I wish I had made a different choice that would have led to more adventure and greater life experiences. But it's pretty unrealistic to think a forty-something with a husband and two kids can suddenly pick up, go back to an out-of-state college, and join a sorority!

On the other hand, one of my life's wishes has been to own a weekend home on a lake. I felt that doing so would bring me a lot of peace, more time together with my family, and personal happiness. I felt that with hard work, it was something I could realistically achieve. It meant dramatically changing the way I was spending money, but it was doable. I was keeping my wishes well within my reach.

This is not to say you shouldn't set your sights high; I'm all about dreaming big. Some of the most successful entrepreneurs in the business world were told over and over that their wishes would never come true, and yet they persevered in spite of the naysayers. That's because they knew they had control over many of the things necessary to achieve success. They had confidence, courage, and conviction. They worked at building connections with other people who could help. And they were committed to doing the hard work and making the sacrifices to bring their ideas to fruition. Apply these same principles to your own wish list, and I guarantee you will see results.

GUIDELINE #2: MAKE WISHES COURAGEOUSLY

I often see people limiting themselves when it comes to making wishes for a better life because they are afraid of change. I completely understand this. As human beings, we are creatures of habit. We like the safeness of our routines. We find the things that work for us, and we stick to them. But it's time to start power-wishing. I highly recommend courageous thinking when it comes to your wish list. Long ago, I knew that if I was going to be powered by happy, I would need to make gutsy changes at a few points in my life, and I've never regretted them. The predictions I made of terrible consequences never came true; I was merely wrestling with the fear in my head. In one of my favorite books, *Feel the Fear and Do It Anyway*, author Susan Jeffers tells her readers that there's no such thing as a wrong decision because of the personal growth you will always experience from any change. I agree. Here's a personal story of how I made a big change I wished for in my life.

Years ago, I found myself in a terrible work situation. While I had a great title (I was a senior vice-president for a multibillion-dollar corporation) and made great money (my bonuses were, for lack of a better term, "stupid good"), I was miserable. I worked more than fifty hours a week every week, and travel started to take up more and more of my time. Before I knew it, I was spending more than 50 percent of my time out of town. I quickly realized that I had made a terrible mistake by taking on this position. Even though the job looked great from the outside, it wasn't fulfilling any of my personal needs. I was missing time with my kids, husband, and friends because I was glued to my desk.

The job was a bad fit all around. The culture was intense and workaholic-oriented. It took me away from what I loved and made me resent my work. Even though I've always been the type of person to finish work in less time than expected, I found myself feeling pressured to be at the office to put in "face time." And in the rare instances when I was able to sneak away from the office, I wondered if people were talking about my absence.

I knew I had a choice: I could stick the job out, using the money I earned to give my kids lots of possessions and fancy trips, or I could look for another job. I knew there had to be a job out there that would fulfill me and also provide me with an environment in which my personality would thrive. Luckily, I had been smart about never "living up to my income" and had saved some money.

So I did something most people would think was crazy. I walked away from my fancy job and took a job that paid me half the salary. Yes, half. And I gave up my bonuses. Why? Because I found a job where the CEO was more focused on results than face time, where morals, values, and integrity were valued, and where everyone was encouraged to have a work/life balance.

This was my own courageous wish I fulfilled to have more time with my family, no matter what it meant to my own career. They came first. I never looked back and never had one regret. And guess what? Within a year, I was back to making my salary from before. The difference was that I finally had the time to enjoy it with my family.

GUIDELINE #3: MAKE SURE YOU DON'T RUSH YOUR WISHES ALONG

We live in times when instant gratification is expected all too often. My grandparents never dreamed of the technological advances we have today that let us perform everyday tasks at the speed of light. My parents labored for years to save money for things we expect to have within months of their appearance on the market. This generation's "gotta have it now" mentality can really trip you up as you try to plan for a more satisfying life. Remember that the things on your wish list aren't likely to be overnight sensations. I believe that anything worthwhile is not just worth waiting for; it's worth working for.

A former colleague of mine had "I wish to own a successful business that's fulfilling to me and to the people who work for me" on his wish list for many years. In the beginning, he worked a regular job and began a freelance business on the side. After a few years, he was able to work in the business as its sole employee. A few more years passed, and he was able to add two employees. They experienced some tough years, and there were times when he worried about making the payroll. They worked harder, and two employees grew to twelve. Today his company employs several hundred people, and it's thriving. It's a wish come true. It took years. But most of all, it took patience.

Another friend of mine recently learned about giving her wishes time to come true. A year into her marriage, she found herself absolutely desperate to have a baby. She was obsessed with the idea, to the point where she was forcing her body to have symptoms even though she was never pregnant. She was so focused on getting pregnant that she began to develop higher levels of stress and anxiety. Then one day she realized that her obsession with getting pregnant was probably what was preventing her from getting pregnant.

So even though it meant putting her wish on the back burner, she decided to refocus her attention on enjoying the first few years of her marriage and let the pregnancy come on its own. She realized that by letting her body relax, she'd not only be happier but also more likely to become pregnant. Learning to step back and look at her wish like this has been immensely helpful—both for her health and for her marriage.

WISHES TAKE WORK: WHAT TO DO TO MAKE YOURS COME TRUE

If I were to rewrite the lyrics to that Disney tune, it would probably go something like, "When you wish upon a star, have a plan or you won't go far!" As I've said here, making wishes come true takes work. Bringing more happiness into your life requires a plan. And this is where you can connect that wish list back to your daily to-do list. After you have come up with a solid wish list, you can start to identify the specific actions that will help you make your wishes come true.

Later in this chapter, you'll get the chance to begin crafting your own personal wish list. But first I'll show you an example of my wish list, along with the specific actions I've taken (or am still taking!) to ensure I achieve success. Here's my wish list from several years ago:

• I wish that my parents will live a long, happy life and that I'll be there for them along the way.

- I wish to be the head of learning for a major corporation so I can help others learn and grow in their careers.

- I wish to become a nationally recognized expert on the topic of learning and training so I can inspire others to improve their training programs and help their employees.

- I wish to have two or three kids.

- I wish to own a vacation home where I can find peace, serenity, and happiness with myself and with my family.

- I wish to be remembered as the best mother, wife, and friend, who was wise, supportive, and loving.

- I wish to be able to provide financially for my children to attend college so they are free of debt and able to focus fully on their own learning and growth.

- I wish to retire by the time I am fifty-five so my husband and I can enjoy life together without financial pressure.

- I wish to go to heaven when I die and help my family get there, too.

So how about a progress report? From the wishes I listed several years ago, I'm happy to report I've achieved a lot of them. True, the jury is still out on being the best mother, wife, and friend. And someone else will be the judge of the heaven thing! Sadly, my wish for a long and happy life for my parents didn't come true. Though both of my beloved parents have since passed away, I experienced a lot of happiness with them in their final years. Caring for them during their illnesses also taught me to appreciate their lives, their legacies, and the memories they left behind for my family to enjoy for years to come.

There's no question that my wish list evolved as I grew in my career and in my role as a mother. I've since added and subtracted a few things; there were detours and side trips along the way. But having a well-thought-out plan for making my wishes come true and a to-do list that helped me get there made it possible for me to reach many of my goals.

Looking back at my wishes, here are some of the to-dos I tackled that helped me get there:

- I met with a financial planner and mapped out my financial goals. We created a savings plan so I could achieve them.

- I focused the work I accepted in the learning field on best practices and always positioned myself as "speedy" or "unique," a person who got the job done on time and with extraordinary quality.

- I strived to be the person who took risks and would offer new and exciting ways to learn. I volunteered for projects that were highly visible and critical to my organization.

- I found a mentor to help navigate my career and teach me how to be an executive.

* I organized my career (and even left a few jobs) so I was able to spend the most time with my kids, husband, and friends.

* I read books and spent time with other mothers I admired to learn from their positive parenting tips.

* I scheduled regular one-on-one activities with my husband and each of my daughters so we could build our relationships in a healthy way.

* I became active in my church and brought God into our lives at every opportunity.

What happens to people that make a wish list at work? Does it help get them through the day? Does it help bring focus to their career? Does it help motivate them to strive for something better? Yes, yes, and yes! Having goals or wishes at work is incredibly important for you to plan out your career, to help you achieve what truly makes you happy there. You won't become CEO overnight; you won't get your boss's job just because you want it. You have to plan. A wish list for your career can help you do just that.

THE GREATEST WISH OF ALL: WISHING TO BE REMEMBERED WELL

When I talk to others about building their wish list, I try not to dictate what should be included. Hopes and dreams, after all, are deeply personal. Yours might revolve around your professional life, your desire to explore the world, or your need to stay closer to home with friends and family. At the same time, there's one idea I think everyone should consider when articulating wishes for happiness: the wish to be remembered in a certain way after they're gone.

This is a powerful idea. To be able to plan now for how you want to be remembered later is an opportunity few people grasp. Once again, the chaos of daily living keeps us so busy that we forget to reflect on such a profound and important connection to happiness. This is your chance to make the most of such a wonderful opportunity to plan the legacy you want to leave behind. What could make us happier than knowing that we achieved something great with our lives, that we made a difference, that we touched others, that we left behind a path that others will want to follow?

I once saw a doctor interviewed on TV about his experiences working with patients who were in hospice care and facing the end of their lives. Over the years, he found there were remarkably consistent themes in his conversations with them. The questions his patients often asked were, "Was I loved and did I love others?" and "Did I make a difference?" This hit me like a ton of bricks. I realized then that exploring in the present how you want to be remembered in the future is something each of us should consider while we have the chance. It's the ultimate wish for your list.

My friends, family members, and I have had many fascinating

discussions about this idea. Here are some of the inspiring things I've heard from them during these discussions:

- "I wish to be remembered for the compassion I showed to others who were hurting."

- "I wish to be remembered as a great coach—at the office, with the kids I coached in soccer, and with others who needed my help."

- "I wish to be remembered as someone who built a company that prevailed long after I was gone and kept many others employed and able to support their families."

- "I wish to be remembered as the most amazing mom."

- "I wish to be remembered as someone who could always be counted on to deliver."

- "I wish to be remembered as someone who made people laugh."

No one understood this concept better than seventeen-year-old Miles Levin from Bloomfield Hills, Michigan. Miles was diagnosed with cancer in his teen years and battled it for some time. His mother, Nancy—fulfilling her own wish to devote herself to Miles's recovery—quit her job to care for him full-time. Rather than spend time feeling sorry for himself, Miles knew instinctively that his illness, however challenging, provided him with the opportunity to make a difference with his life. He started a blog and posted frequent messages about his journey, his deepest thoughts and fears, and even his optimism about facing his illness. More than fifteen thousand people read it daily. It inspired hundreds of people to reach out to him with messages, with God's blessings, and with encouragement. It provided comfort not just to him but to many others.

Miles ultimately lost his battle with cancer. But shortly before his death, he stopped wishing to be cured and instead courageously wished for his illness to mean something to others. In the last words published before his death, he wrote, "Dying is not what scares me; it's dying having had no impact. I know a lot of eyes are watching me suffer, and—win or lose—this is my time for impact." In the end, Miles had nothing to fear. I believe his life did have impact. Reading this means that now you too can be one of the thousands of people whom Miles impacted.

The late author and columnist Erma Bombeck wrote about her regrets in a poem I like to read occasionally when I've lost perspective on what's important in life. In "If I Had My Life to Live Over," she describes what she would change if she could replay her life again. She wishes she had talked less and listened more. With the chance to do it all again, she'd have let go of the little things, like getting stains on her pants from sitting in the grass, getting windblown hair from driving in a convertible, or worrying about eating popcorn on the "good" furniture in the living room. She would have said more "I love yous" and "I'm sorrys." Toward the end of the poem, she tells her readers to stop sweating the small stuff and to quit worrying about who doesn't like them. Instead, she writes, "Let's cherish the relationships we do have with those who love us."

Both Miles and Erma wished to be remembered as those whose enduring words of wisdom inspired others to change their lives for the better.

REMEMBERED AT THE OFFICE

How do you wish to be remembered at work? As a powerful executive? As a drill sergeant? As a micromanager? What you do today can never be taken away, but what you do tomorrow can change. Make a commitment to yourself and to those who work around you to be kind, to be a coach, to be a leader, and to be respectful. These are the professional attributes that I would want said in my eulogy.

Do you work hard or hardly work? Are there ever times that you "wish" you did something different at work? Are there times when it is too late to change something? I think not, not if you are reading this book. It's never too late to wish for something good to happen. If you have made mistakes, if you have offended a colleague, if you have not given it your all at work, it's not too late to wish for things to get better and tackle the to-dos to make it happen.

And now that we've talked about how to write your own

personal wish list, let's get to it! Be sure to think about the things that will be most impactful to you and your long-term happiness.

EXERCISE: WRITING YOUR WISH LIST

STEP ONE
In the space below, write down the five wishes you feel would help you lead a happier, more fulfilling life:

_____

_____

_____

_____

_____

STEP TWO
Now look at your wish list. What are the things you must do and the steps you must take to help make your wishes come true? Prepare the list of to-do items that will help you get there:

_____

_____

_____

_____

_____

Now that you have made the first draft of your own personal wish list, set it aside for a few days before you revisit it. Make changes and revisions, if necessary. Share it with people who know you well and ask for their thoughts. Then get going with your plan to put it into action. You're now on your way to a life filled with greater happiness, one where all your wishes come true!

HAPPINESS P.S.

Here's something to ponder: what have you done lately to help someone else's wish come true? Try asking! Pick a friend or family member, and learn what they've been wishing for. See what you can do to make a difference. It's a great feeling.

:)

TAKE THE "UN" OUT OF "UNHAPPY" AND BE GRATEFUL

What makes you unhappy?

Until I started to write this book, I can honestly say that I hadn't spent much time thinking about being unhappy. I have always valued putting my focus on the positive rather than the negative. So devoting time to thinking about things that make me unhappy always seemed like an unproductive activity. But what if ignoring the things that make me unhappy was actually hurting my chances of being truly happy?

By deliberately ignoring the things that make me unhappy, was I robbing myself of the chance to resolve them and become even happier? We all know people who represent the opposite of this book's title. Every day, their lives are actually powered by their unhappiness. They like to complain, they focus on what's wrong rather than what's right, and they find comfort in feeling victimized. If you work with someone powered by unhappiness, you know what I'm talking about.

They complain about the boss, the team, the job, the hours, the pay, the assignments, and even the food in the cafeteria. Frankly, it's a vicious cycle to break. But identifying and eliminating the "un" from your life or your team at work can help you find untapped sources of happiness.

GOING FROM UNHAPPY TO HAPPY— JUST SAY THANKS!

Psychologists from the University of California, Davis, conducted a study on gratitude and thankfulness. They divided hundreds of people into three groups: one group recorded daily events, another recorded daily hassles, and the third recorded what they were grateful for. The last group reported more alertness and optimism and better progress toward their goals. They also felt more loved.

In this chapter, I want to help you discover the things that truly make you unhappy and teach you some strategies for addressing them. At the same time, I'll share what I think a little thing like gratefulness has to do with all this.

HOW IS UNHAPPINESS DEFINED?

Here are four answers I have found when I Googled "unhappiness":

1. Sadness; emotions experienced when not in a state of well-being

2. A state characterized by emotions ranging from mild discontentment to deep grief

3. The feeling of not being happy

4. A feeling caused by the belief that happiness lies in outside things rather than in your own thinking and state of mind

But while these definitions cover the scientific and general principles of a word we're all familiar with, they don't explain that unhappiness can mean something different to each of us. Our first exercise in this chapter will be defining unhappiness in our own terms.

EXERCISE: WHAT MAKES YOU UNHAPPY?

For me, the word unhappiness refers to the feeling I get when my kids are troubled, when I feel bad about myself or my appearance, when I feel overwhelmed or stressed about my responsibilities, and when my relationships are not in line. I can feel unhappy because of a situation, a particular problem, or just because I woke up on the wrong side of the bed.

Now it's your turn. On the next few lines, write down what generally defines unhappiness for you. Feel free to write down a situation or problem that is causing your unhappiness as well.

Unhappiness to me is _____
_____
_____
_____

Let's take it a step further. In the space below, write three things that make you unhappy and, for each, write a strategy you will develop to improve it.

What Makes Me Unhappy	How to Turn It Around

Let's take a work example.

Problem: You are unhappy because one of your colleagues drives you CRAZY, has a bad attitude toward you, and brings you down literally every day.

Strategy: Take this person out to lunch and address this with him or her head-on. Give the person specifics. Explain that when he or she does [insert action], you feel [insert emotion]. Ask if there is something you have done to upset this person. Explain that having a good working relationship with him or her is important to you. You don't have to be your colleague's best friend, but friction in the office is the cause of much unhappiness in work environments today. If this is one of the causes of your unhappiness, solving it will go a long way toward increasing your joy at work.

Need some help coming up with strategies? Keep reading.

BECOME A BETTER JUGGLER—AND OTHER TIPS FOR DEALING WITH UNHAPPINESS

The first thing you have to do is make peace with what makes you unhappy. Give yourself some attention. To do this, try this exercise:

* **Become aware of what you are feeling in the moment.** Set a timer for five minutes to intensely feel whatever you're feeling. For example, if you are sad, allow yourself to cry. When the timer goes off, get up and get on with your day.

* **Challenge long-held beliefs about what will make you happy.** Reread chapter 1, if you need to, to get a better handle on what will really make your heart sing.

* **Become a better juggler.** A common reason for unhappiness is stress, and a vast majority of Americans feel stressed by their responsibilities. So how can you find happiness in the midst of all your stress? By juggling! Here are some tips for becoming a better juggler:

  • **Do what is counterintuitive.** When you are feeling overwhelmed and too many balls are in the air, stop.

Take twenty minutes and center yourself with a walk, a jog, or even meditation.

- **Do nothing.** Schedule twenty minutes a day for doing nothing. A rest from constant "doing" can help you be more productive when you are working.

- **Just say no!** Decline any nonessential requests requiring your time.

- **Prioritize.** Make a list of everything you need to do, with your most stressful items at the top. Work from the top of your list, and check things off as you accomplish them. This in itself will make you feel better.

- **Make a schedule and stick to it.** Writing each event or item down will help you remember it, and you'll be more prepared for each event.

- **Escape what I call "mood hijacking."** We covered this a little in chapter 3, but it's so important I'm bringing it up again. Do not allow a negative event or thought to bring your whole hour, day, or even week down. Here are some tips for maintaining control of your mood:

  - **Analyze your emotions.** Be aware of what is going on in your body. Are you holding tension in your jaw, or are you getting tense in your upper back? Listen to what your body is telling you—it's usually right!

- **Plan a wise response.** Look for solutions that allow you to face bad situations without getting bogged down in negativity. Think of the positive elements that can come out of each situation.

- **Practice laughing.** Put on a funny video, or read something that delights you every day. You'll appreciate the endorphins as much as you enjoy the movie or book. The more you laugh, the easier it will become. Before you know it, you'll be laughing all the time.

Not only can these tips make you feel happier, but they can make others feel happy, too. That alone can help reverse your unhappiness.

THE POWER OF GRATITUDE

One of the best ways to eliminate unhappiness is so powerful that I'm devoting an entire section to it. And that's gratitude.

Being grateful and appreciative for what's all around is a recurring attribute mentioned by people who consider themselves happy. This is an attribute that we are all capable of cultivating. The things that upset us tend to melt away in the face of gratefulness; it's kryptonite for unhappiness.

A THANK-YOU A DAY KEEPS THE DOCTOR AWAY

Need another reason to cultivate an attitude of gratitude? It's good for your health! Let's look at an excerpt from *Why Good Things Happen to Good People* by Stephen Post on why giving thanks is good for your health:

- **Gratitude defends.** Just fifteen minutes a day focusing on the things you're grateful for will significantly increase your body's natural antibodies.

- **Gratitude sharpens.** Naturally grateful people are more focused mentally and measurably less vulnerable to clinical depression.

- **Gratitude calms.** A grateful state of mind induces a physiological state called resonance that's associated with healthier blood pressure and heart rate.

- **Gratitude strengthens.** Caring for others is draining. But grateful caregivers are healthier and more capable than less grateful ones.

- **Gratitude heals.** Recipients of donated organs who have the most grateful attitudes heal faster.

GRATITUDE LETS YOU ENJOY THE SIMPLE GOOD

Gratitude allows you to enjoy the good in your life. Often we feel that we will only be happy after achieving the big goals—like getting the big promotion, winning the lottery, or having the best party. But focusing on being appreciative allows you to focus on the many small good things in your day that you are grateful for, such as being on time for the bus, getting your favorite drink in the vending machine, seeing a beautiful sky, sharing a laugh with your partner, or seeing your kids healthy and happy and playing. These things make life very enjoyable and satisfying, but often we take them for granted in our search for the big and flashy successes. Practicing gratitude allows us to appreciate our success and our happiness more.

This is pretty easy to do when things are going well. It's not as easy when things get tough. I find those days the most challenging, but also the most rewarding. Every night at dinner (when my family is fortunate enough to actually eat together), we go around the table and say one thing we are grateful for that happened that day. It really helps our day end on a good note and even makes the horrible days appear not so bad.

Try it at the office: challenge yourself and your colleagues to name what you're grateful for at work. Not only will it make all of you feel a little better about work, but it might also inspire you and others to find even more reasons to feel grateful at work. In a down economic climate, you will hear many people say, "I'm just grateful to have a job." The next time someone says that, drill into it a bit. Find out what specifically they are grateful for. Being grateful for your job is great, but being grateful about specific attributes or even people you work with will not only help enhance your happiness at work but also give you a stronger drive to protect that job and perhaps even perform better.

GET GRATITUDE WORKING FOR YOU

If you enjoy your job, make your gratitude work for you. Think about the impact or impression you are making on others, maybe even on those who have the power to promote you. Organizations thrive on positive, energetic people who are passionate about what they do. People who are positive and grateful are the employees who are first to be promoted. Being unhappy can be career-limiting, but most people don't realize this until it is too late.

If you don't enjoy your job and you are having trouble finding anything to be grateful for, don't worry! You can take control of your situation and make it better. I had a job where I enjoyed the work I did, the team I managed, and 99 percent of the colleagues I worked with, but the culture and my manager made my job a living hell. Every day before I went to work, I had a pit in my stomach. I dreaded leaving the house and sometimes cried before I went to work. It was a horrible time for me, mostly because I had to pretend to be happy. I let my unhappiness at work become a huge issue that I couldn't seem to get control over. I felt like I was in a situation that seemed to get worse every single day.

Then one day some great advice from an old friend came crashing into my head: If you died tomorrow, who would miss you the most? That's easy, I thought to myself: my family and friends. Answering this question took my attention off all of my complaints about my job and reminded me of how lucky I really was. I have a great family, and my friends are the best. When

I refocused my energy on my gratitude for what I had and the support I was lucky enough to enjoy at home, I was able to clear my head about what needed to be done. Yes, I hated my job, but it wasn't the worst thing in the world. All around me I saw people struggling with illness, unemployment, financial worries, and divorces. When I saw that my work situation was, in fact, a small problem compared with the things millions of people deal with daily, I was able to put my job problems in perspective. Being unhappy at work wasn't a problem that was going to kill me. It was just something I needed to deal with.

With my new perspective on my career, I took control of my destiny and started to look for jobs. But instead of letting it overwhelm me and add to my stress, I would simply repeat the phrase "It's just a job" to myself. I would remember that people all over the world have much bigger and more frightening problems to deal with, and many of them have no control over what will happen to them. When I thought of my job hunt as just another part of my life, I found that I could think clearly and rationally about what I wanted. As soon as I put this all into perspective, I got another career opportunity that not only challenged me every day but allowed me to focus on my family and friends more than I ever have.

GRATITUDE REDUCES ENVY AND NEGATIVE EMOTION

When you are busy appreciating and savoring all the good things already in your life, there is little time to hanker for what others have. Take a simple, common, materialistic example: Let's you say you have a regular twenty-inch TV, but you want one of those newfangled flat-screen plasma items to watch the big game on. You keep thinking of how great it would be to see the game on that big screen and how you wish you had it. You focus on how unsatisfying watching the game on your TV will be. You feel envious of your neighbor's big TV, and this makes you feel bad about yourself.

Now imagine instead that you focus on appreciating the fact that you have a TV to watch the game on. You appreciate that it is your own TV and that you can watch it while sitting in your favorite chair. You are satisfied and appreciative of the TV you have, rather than being unhappy and wishing you had another one. See the difference? In each scenario, the facts are the same: you have a small TV, and you want to watch the game. But with an attitude of gratitude, the second scenario is positive from start to finish. Being grateful helps reduce envy and resentment, and it also promotes satisfaction and happiness.

How many times have you been jealous of someone at work? Perhaps a colleague is getting more attention than you. Perhaps she got the promotion you deserved. Perhaps he always gets the "easy" sales. When you spend more time focusing on others and being envious, it reflects in the work you do and how you appear to others. When you let the ugly green monster come out, others can see that, and it is not a good reflection of you at the office. People can see right through it; they can see the envy and your negative attitude. This is surely a way to change your career—change it to the unemployment line! If you flip the energy you are spending on envy and negative emotion to what you have to be thankful for and what you are contributing to the company, you will be noticed in a much more positive light—and maybe get the change in your career that is up the ladder instead of out the door.

GRATITUDE IMPROVES YOUR EMOTIONAL WELL-BEING

Gratitude isn't just physically helpful; it can improve your emotional life as well. Gratitude helps you transform even the most negative events into tools for becoming stronger. People who focus on gratitude can achieve closure and recover faster from negative events because they focus their attention on growth, rather than pain.

As you go through your day, practice being aware of the many good things in life. Never mind if it feels corny; just do it. Simple things such as your good health, your family, and your friends are things to be thankful for. Try to focus on those things and acknowledge how grateful you are to have them in your life. If you're having trouble brainstorming about things to be grateful for, take a look at some of the things my friends are grateful for:

- "I'm thankful that in our poor economic climate, I still have a job and am still receiving a paycheck and benefits to take care of my family."

- "I'm thankful that my job provides me with a great challenge and a great opportunity to move up in my career."

- "I'm thankful God's got us covered. Even when we don't see it, feel it, hear it from others, we can still believe it. I've lost my job but gained more time. My health is hurting, but I know where my focus needs to be. The future is uncertain but never bleak with a thankful heart."

- "Six years ago, my husband was told I would not live to see the next day. I'm not grateful that my life is difficult, being unable to drive, work, walk, or use my left arm anymore. I am, however, grateful to all the friends and family who have helped me in my time of need. God has been very good to me in the midst of difficult circumstances. I don't know how people can survive without God in their lives!"

- "Every morning on my ride into work, I place the radio on low on a spa music channel and recite out loud all my blessings that my family and I receive along with the ones to come: health, love, friends, family, a job, and a home. Then I bless my family and friends. It puts the whole day into perspective."

EXERCISE: THANKS FOR...

Whether it's something little—like the fact that you made it to work on time—or something big—like the fact that your children are healthy—focusing on things you are grateful for can help usher your unhappiness out the door. Here are some simple tips to help you feel grateful every day:

• Include giving thanks in your bedtime ritual with your kids.

• Appreciate people every day. Tell them what a good job they are doing—even if it's writing the maid at your hotel a note thanking her for cleaning your room.

• Write to a person that has made a difference in your life, and share how grateful you are for him or her.

Let's try it now. Either mentally list the things you're grateful for, or write them down. Start with this simple sentence, and see how the start of your day will change.

I am thankful for _____

_____

_____

_____

_____

_____

_____

Once you start focusing on the things you are grateful for, you will begin to see a whole new side of life. You'll learn to reprogram your brain, and instead of hunting out the worst-case scenarios, you'll find yourself noticing things to be thankful for that you've never even seen before!

Make it a goal that every time you are feeling unhappy, you think of one thing you are grateful for. Doing this exercise over and over again will change your behavior and become a habit, so that you will limit the time you spend thinking unhappy thoughts and increase your gratitude for all the good things in your life.

THE VALUE OF WHAT YOU'RE GRATEFUL FOR

Here's an interesting way to look at the intertwined relationships between happiness, unhappiness, and gratitude: once you've thought about what you're grateful for, think about the importance you're giving it in your life.

If the very things you're most grateful for play a small part in your daily life, you may have found the roots of some unhappiness.

I want to tell you a story about a colleague of mine from the Limited Brands. He held the position of CFO and worked seventy hours a week. He was the first one to come in and the last one to leave work every day, although he had two little girls at home he never saw. If you were sitting on my side of his desk, he appeared to have it all: great living, great company, great position, and great control over his life. I assumed he loved it. One day as I was leaving the office, I told him the story of how my dad worked so hard that it eventually killed him. I poured my heart out about how my dad didn't get to see his retirement, and it's one of the saddest things I have to deal with in life. We had a pretty intense chat, and he told me how much he missed his girls; he felt like soon they would be off to college and wouldn't even know him.

Weeks later, I heard through the grapevine that he had resigned. What? I ran in to question him, and he said that our conversation was so impactful that he started to evaluate what was truly making him unhappy and then what he was most grateful for. The one thing that was making him the most unhappy—his time spent in the office—was the one thing that held him back from the things he was most grateful for—his daughters. So he quit, became a teacher, and spent the summers and weekends coaching his girls' sports. He is a much happier and more grateful man today because of that brave move. It changed his life.

How can it change yours?

HAPPINESS P.S.

Eileen Caddy wrote, "Gratitude helps you to grow and expand; gratitude brings joy and laughter into your life and into the lives of all of those around you." Sometimes it can be hard to generate a gracious attitude, but just think about the people in your life who can benefit from your gratitude.

:)

MAKE A HIGH-YIELD HAPPINESS INVESTMENT

When we think about how to become happier, our thoughts normally center on ourselves. We think in terms of "me," "I," and "myself" because, well, it seems like the obvious place to start. But what if you started to look around you? Could you boost your own happiness by investing in the happiness of others? You bet!

HAPPINESS NOTE CARD: THE ONE CHEAP THING THAT WILL MAKE SOMEONE HAPPY EVERY TIME

Making others happy doesn't need to cost you a lot of money or even time. A simple compliment or a listening ear can go a long way. Here are some examples of what my friends said made their days:

- "The time my boss spends coaching me on how to become a better professional"

- "A colleague taking the time out of their busy day to check in on me and offer help where needed"

- "Advice from my mentor in helping me accomplish my goals"

- "Hearing from someone at work, 'Great job'"

- "A simple thank-you from a friend for being an inspiration during a difficult time"

- "Helping a friend get connected to a company where he was able to find a job"

- "Sending an anonymous note to someone going through a difficult time to let the person know you care"

- "Giving a compliment to a complete stranger"

- "Getting a smile from a colleague at work and saying, 'Have a great day'"

- "Giving a gift card to a friend in need"

- "Helping children cope with their problems"

In my research on happiness, I have found that a great way to sustain long-term happiness is to help those in need. In this chapter, you'll discover the importance of giving to others, how giving anonymously can contribute to the happiness of many, and how you can start giving today.

HOW INVESTING IN SOMEONE ELSE'S HAPPINESS CONTRIBUTES TO YOURS

At work, how much time do you spend making yourself successful? Think about your day. In eight hours, how much time do you spend on your work, your boss, or your customers? I'm sure many of you will say all eight, if not nine, ten, eleven, or twelve hours. At the end of the day, it's likely you are pretty exhausted, even more so when you think about getting up and doing it all over again. What if, however, you spent thirty minutes a day helping someone else be successful? Sharing a best practice or lesson learned? Offering to be a mentor or coach to a new young professional? Helping a colleague with a presentation he or she is struggling with? Giving advice, lending an ear, or taking out members of your staff to talk about how much you value their contributions? If you did this every day, or at least three times a week, do you think you would feel different at the end of your day? Could it perhaps give you an extra bounce in your step? It's worth the time investment to use the knowledge, skills, and abilities that you have to help someone else to get another level.

I have found in my career that when this happens, it can come back to you threefold.

Let's take a little example. I was featured in an article in *Fast Company* magazine in July 1999, portrayed as the "Queen of Training," crown and all. Even now, remembering the photo shoot in the Limited Brands cafe makes me smile. I was thrilled to be in such a prestigious magazine. (My husband actually said, after seeing folks like business book author and marketing guru Seth Godin in it, "What the heck are you doing in the magazine, with such a big spread to boot?") Anyway, after being in the magazine, I received over six hundred emails from across the world, from complete strangers, asking for advice: How did I do it? What was my experience? My education? What advice did I have for them?

You know what? I responded to every single email with humility. I first thanked each person for taking the time to reach out and answered any question he or she had. After that, I received an incredible amount of emails from people who just wanted to say "thanks" for my responses. Nobody expected it, yet the happiness it gave me to know I'd helped them in even a small way lasted years—and as you can see, the gratitude is still there, as I remembered to write about it even today, several years later.

It's not just about helping others in the professional world. I have found that in general, helping people or organizations in need rounds out our giving to make us better people.

Here's a bigger example. Recently I was on my way to do some furniture shopping with a friend, which I thought was our way of single-handedly boosting the economy. As I was getting out of my car, my friend received a call from Joe, her friend Anna's husband.

Joe used to have it all. He had a thriving business, a happy marriage, and beautiful children. But then his business took a turn for the worse, and his revenue went from millions to close to nothing. Finally, he was forced to close its doors. After his dream died, so did part of Joe. He turned to drugs and alcohol, and he eventually wound up in rehab. Just when it seemed as though he'd hit rock bottom, his health began to fail. It got so bad that one day Anna called my friend to say that the priest was reading Joe his last rites and their children were saying their final good-byes.

Miraculously, Joe came out of it, and after months of rehabilitation, he was soon back at home, fighting for the peace he was missing in his life. Joe got a job, and Anna took on several part-time jobs to make ends meet. But they were barely making it. Then the bottom fell out of the economy, and Joe was once again unemployed and desperate. Watching Joe and his family survive ordeal after ordeal was heartbreaking, and my friend stood by them throughout it all, constantly telling them that she would do whatever she could to help them get on their feet again. Whether it was financial or emotional support—or just being there to listen to their worries—she was committed to helping our friends survive.

This brings me back to Joe's phone call. As I sat in the parking lot of a furniture store, ready to drop a few thousand dollars on a new living-room set, Joe asked my friend if he could borrow five hundred dollars to pay a debt. I heard my friend say, without hesitation, "Of course. Whatever you need." She called the debt collector right from the store, pretending to be Joe's sister, and paid his bills. After the transaction was done, the woman at the debt collection agency quietly said to my friend, "You are an awful nice sister."

Joe offered to pay my friend back over the next few weeks, but she didn't want his money. As Joe thanked her, his voice cracking, all I could think of was how hard that call must have been for him to make.

As we walked through the furniture store, my friend cried. They were tears of sadness for her dear friends but also tears of happiness. My friend felt grateful to have been able to help such good and deserving people.

There are Joes and Annas all around us—people who seemed to have it all but are now in need. My friend was willing to give because Joe and Anna were so generous when they were successful, when they did have it all. Those are the people we want to help when they are in need.

If you are successful right now, how are *you* living your life? If you suddenly lost your job or went through a personal tragedy, would others feel the need to help you?

My friend who helped Joe and Anna is a CIO of a Fortune 500 company, and seeing her do this so willingly made me respect her as an executive, and, even more importantly, as a human being. This is the type of executive I would work for in an instant. She is a leader who cares about people.

What inspires us to care as leaders? What motivates us, as employees, to sacrifice for those leaders? Think about our men and woman at war. I am in awe of them. They are the unspoken heroes of our world. They willingly give up their lives to protect us and to protect their country. Transfer this to leadership: what do leaders have to do to make us want to sacrifice for our company and our company's success? They need to care.

I work with several leaders in top companies around the country, and their ability to care inside and outside the office helps them gain the respect of their subordinates. They are willing to make sacrifices when needed to boost their performance and their company's success. What type of leader are you? What are your employees willing to do for you?

A HOT INVESTMENT TIP FOR EVERYONE

Giving to others can help us take stock of our busy lives and realize just how big a difference a small act can make. The other day, my friend Ellen, a senior vice-president at Chase, was rushing around running errands. As she was hurrying through the grocery store, a complete stranger complimented her on how nice she looked. Now, Ellen always looks like a million dollars, but this little act of kindness took her completely off guard. She was so impressed by this stranger's kindness that it made her whole day a little brighter.

Think about how this plays out at work. How do you feel when you receive words of encouragement and recognition for your hard work? Doesn't it power up your day and make you feel like you can do just about anything? Throughout my career, I have learned and also felt that when those annual performance reviews come around, the words on the review meant more than the money I would receive. (Truthfully, that was perhaps later in my career, rather than when I was just starting out and really needed the extra fifty cents an hour!) This is the same sentiment I've heard from many of my colleagues and trusted advisors over the years. Words of encouragement are meaningful not only from a complete stranger in a grocery store but also from your boss, your direct reports, and your peers. Think about making someone's day by sharing what you value and appreciate about his or her contributions. As a leader, remember to reward and recognize often and sincerely; the productivity you will receive back from those associates will pay you back tenfold. It doesn't cost you a thing, but it is one of the only no-fail investments you will ever make.

We often think that in order to make a difference in some-one's life, we need to make grandiose gestures, like starting a charity or raising thousands of dollars for AIDs research. But it's just as important to take advantage of the little opportunities to brighten someone's day.

This chapter will provide a variety of suggestions for improving the lives of others through gifts of your time, skills, and money. But if you're still stumped on how you can give, check out the websites helpothers.org and actsofkindness.org.

"A" IS FOR ANONYMOUS

The Bible tells us that we should give with a generous heart and not one that is seeking recognition. In other words, don't donate to charity or give money to your local Girl Scout troop just so that people can see how wealthy and important you are. If you are looking to give only to gain something in return, you are giving for the wrong reasons. Giving money or time or goods so that you can be recognized for it is not an investment that will pay you the dividends you want. Sure, you might feel proud and important seeing yourself on that "donors" list, but it won't last. If you're looking for true happiness, you're going to have to rethink your strategy for giving.

Giving anonymously isn't just for the Rockefellers among us. In fact, it's something we can all do to achieve higher levels of happiness. Giving anonymously gives you a better return on your investment because it takes away any chance of making the recipient feel embarrassed. You won't have to worry about anyone questioning your intentions, and you won't have to feel self-conscious about giving your gift. All you will have to do is sit back and enjoy the response.

Not long ago, my church group was taking kids on a youth trip to Nashville, Tennessee, called Winterfest. It's an inspiring weekend. I have taken my daughter on the trip a few times. One year, I overheard a few moms at church saying they would love to take their kids but just couldn't afford the weekend fee. They knew how important the weekend would be for their kids, but they couldn't find a way to stretch their finances to make it work. I could tell that they were sad and humbled that they couldn't offer their children this opportunity.

Then just a few weeks later in our church bulletin, I saw a note that said, "Thank you to the anonymous giver that helped our kids go to Winterfest." Someone had donated enough money to the church to take all the kids. And because it was an anonymous donation, the kids who couldn't afford to go on the weekend trip never had to feel sad or embarrassed about their circumstances, and the parents who were the recipients of the donation never had to feel uncomfortable around their friends. And I'm certain that whoever donated that money enjoyed seeing the happiness of the church community. Though I'm pretty sure I know who this generous donor was, I'll protect her anonymity so that her gift can remain as pure as she intended it to be.

While offering financial help to others is a great way to contribute to your own happiness as well as to the happiness of others, it is by no means the only way to give anonymously. You can give your time by donating old clothing or giving to a soup kitchen. Get creative! There are an infinite number of opportunities to improve someone else's life and reap the rewards at the same time.

EXERCISE: HOW TO HELP

Let's pause for a minute to think about a friend whom you might be able to help. In the spaces below, write down the friend's name and how you believe you can help. Think about what the person is struggling with, how you might be able to assist him or her, and how your help will contribute to his or her happiness. Think about whether you could offer your help anonymously. If so, think about the benefits of helping your friend without him or her knowing that the help came from you. Finally, create a plan to help.

The friend I would like to help is _____

What does this person need help with?

_____

_____

_____

_____

_____

What can I do to help?

_____

_____

_____

_____

_____

How will my help make this person happy?

_____

_____

_____

_____

_____

Can I help this person anonymously?

_____

_____

My plan to help:

_____

_____

_____

_____

GIVING AT THE OFFICE

In the last exercise, you thought about a friend who needed your help and how you are going to offer it. Have you ever thought about offering the same kind of help to your colleagues? Offering help at work can not only help you achieve greater levels of happiness but also make your workplace a more positive environment and encourage other co-workers to help out as well.

Believe it or not, opportunities to help pop up all the time in professional situations. Have you ever had a friend who was unemployed? Have you ever had a friend who was struggling with a boss or colleague? I'm sure you have. While these situations probably sound like the same old work drama you deal with daily, they are actually great opportunities to give.

In this economy, it can seem that we're constantly hearing about people who are losing their jobs. But instead of letting this bad news get you down, turn it around. Look through your contacts to see if you can help out. Recently, an old colleague whom I didn't know very well called me out of the blue. He asked if I could help his daughter find work in a retail store, since she was majoring in fashion and needed the experience. Even though I hadn't talked to this person in years, I used my retail connections to set up an interview for his daughter. I had absolutely nothing to gain from this; still it made me feel great for the rest of the week. I was able to help a young woman in the first stages of what is sure to be a great career.

Another opportunity to help stems from miserable employees. How often do you find yourself at a party listening to people lament about how much they hate their job or their boss or their commute? Sometimes those friends are crying out for help. They may be telling you their miserable stories because they secretly hope you have a solution to give them. So listen and let them vent—it's the best help you can offer.

And if you have that magic bullet that will help their situation, offer it up! They will remember that moment for a long time to come, and hopefully you will, too.

Don't be afraid to formalize this relationship. Do you know how many professionals—young men and women—are dying for a mentor or coach? Wouldn't it have been great if someone approached you early on in your career to offer free help? Reach out to someone you know, and see if he or she would like to meet with you periodically to discuss some career challenges and aspirations. It's a great way to give back at the office. You will be surprised how much it helps you mentally, not to mention that reliving many of your experiences helps you be a better professional, which leadership very much looks upon as a "star" attribute.

Ellen Kindle mentored me at JPMorgan Chase. I asked her what was the most rewarding part of that mentorship. She said, "The satisfaction of knowing that I helped make some of your days a little better and also that I helped protect you from things I didn't know when I started that were painful lessons learned."

I have worked with many executive coaches, and I'd like to share some of the advice I've received from them that has helped me throughout my career.

- **Don't take work personally.** When you get criticized in front of others, separate yourself from the situation. Do not internalize it. Deal with the facts and hold your composure.

The ability to do this is one of the key differences between managers and nonmanagers.

- **Stay focused and organized in meetings or confrontations.** Know what you want the outcome to be before you start. Write key messages down before going into the meeting, and keep these notes in front of you so that if the discussion starts to go in a different direction, you can bring it back, staying focused on your goals.

- **Don't self-promote without a cause.** You certainly want others to know the work you are doing, and at times you absolutely need to promote what you have done. However, do it in a way in which you are not talking about what you have done, but rather about the impact your work has had on your employees or customers. Use "we" more than "I." You will gain much more respect not only from leaders, but also from your direct reports.

- **Show professional courtesy.** Do unto others as you wish to be done to you. If you say you are going to do something, do it. Under-promise and over-deliver. Set appropriate expectations at all times. Respond to your emails timely. Show others respect no matter what their positions.

You don't have to be in a position of management to offer help. One program I have started at work is a peer-to-peer recognition program. This is set up so that peers can nominate peers for a "Way to Go" award. This award is for someone who has gone above and beyond the call of duty to help another person in our office. It is recognized by a card read aloud at our team lunch praising the work the award recipient did, as well as a lunch with the boss or a gift certificate. Hearing a compliment from your boss is one thing but from a peer is sometimes even better!

PAY IT FORWARD

The concept of "paying it forward," the message of a 2000 Kevin Spacey movie, is all about doing good deeds for others in the hopes that they too will do good deeds. In 2007, a coffee shop in Marysville, Washington, saw a community of customers pay it forward. It all started early one morning when a woman getting coffee in the drive-through offered to pay the tab for the car behind her. The car behind her followed suit, and in twenty-four hours, almost five hundred people had joined the cause. The people who bought coffee for perfect strangers that day became a media sensation, inspiring others all over the country to pay it forward.

Six years ago, my husband and I were fortunate to buy a second home near a lake with a boat on the marina. We were "newbies" at the lake, and the marina quickly found out who I was and what my boat looked like (my method of docking the boat was more like crashing the boat). On one of my trips down the dock, complete strangers came up and noticed my two small girls, Madison and Tiffany. They said, "We have skis that no longer fit our kids. Would you like them?" Elated, I said absolutely! I could not believe their generosity and offered to pay them, but of course they didn't want any money. The man simply said, "Pay it forward." This was one of my first experiences with the concept, and every day I try to pay it forward to someone else who may need money, a friend, or advice. Paying it forward doesn't just make you or the recipient of your generosity happy; it makes a whole line of future recipients happy!

How can you "pay it forward" at work? My old boss and now friend Karlin Bohner (VP of Cricket Communications) said that community service is critically important to both her current company and Home Depot (where she was a VP as well). Karlin explained, "Home Depot was very engaged with Habitat for Humanity, and Cricket sponsors Rebuild Together. The fun part of this is that we are able to take our teams out on builds to form team bonding as well as to help others. I don't believe I've seen happier teams than when they complete work and have that feeling of satisfaction from having done a good deed. The teams talked about these events for weeks and weeks after and couldn't wait to get to the next one."

I was recently speaking at a conference on employee engagement for Cornerstone On Demand Software Company, a talent management system. My company partners with CSOD to help companies create not only a talent management strategy but also a system to enable those critical processes. I was struck by a session with the CEO, Adam Miller, in which he discussed the company's philanthropic efforts and how critical it is for the organization to give back—to pay it forward, in a sense. It validated the integrity I saw both in Adam and in his company, which my company also shares. It means a lot to my company to ensure that the partners we deal with have the same morals, values, and integrity that we do.

Does your company have this kind of institutional philanthropy? Can you help instill it?

Knowing this, you can align yourself with the right organization that supports the way you want to behave as a professional. To be fully powered by happy means to constantly look for ways to help those in your company and others in need.

EXERCISE: HOW CAN YOU PAY IT FORWARD?

Has anyone done you a favor lately? It could have been something small, like a stranger opening a door for you, or a colleague giving you a compliment about a big project you just completed. If you think about it hard enough, you're bound to come up with a list of things that people have done for you.

What kind act or favor has someone done for you recently?

_____

_____

_____

Now, brainstorm about how you can pay this favor forward. Write down a kind deed or favor you could do for another person on the lines below. And then pay it forward.

_____

_____

_____

EXERCISE: WHAT KIND OF INVESTOR ARE YOU?

We have talked about several types of "investments" that yield high returns in happiness. However, it is very personal for you to determine what type of investor you are when it comes to giving. Each of us has certain talents that can be shared. My talent, I believe, is my ability to make others laugh. I love that. I have a friend whose talent is her ability to listen. I have another friend who gives great advice on being a mom. You see, these talents don't have to involve acrobatics or nuclear physics. They just have to come from the heart.

The reason I am in the job I am today is because I love to help people. My clients have all become my friends. Most of the friends I speak about in this book are senior executives or employees I have worked with. The funny thing is that as much as I help them, they end up helping me more with their support, advice, and friendship.

This is your time to figure out what talents you have—in or out of the office—that may either brighten someone's day or help a friend in need. Maybe you could bring some of the talents you have outside the office inside the office to help those who need it. I would like you to reflect on what your talents are and how they can be used to help someone else.

My talents are _____

How can these talents help someone in need?

_____

_____

_____

_____

_____

_____

_____

FORTY-PLUS WAYS TO MAKE SOMEONE'S DAY (INCLUDING YOURS!)

As I mentioned before, helping others can be as difficult as giving up your hard-earned money or as simple as giving stranger a nice compliment. It's up to you to figure out what you have to give and how you want to give it.

When thinking of ways you can give, get creative! A few Christmases ago, I wanted to help others but didn't know how. I didn't have any friends who were in need of help, so I asked my sister-in-law, also named Beth, if she knew anyone who was in need. She worked at a private Christian elementary school. Many families were there on scholarships because they couldn't afford the tuition. She quickly responded to me that she knew a family that had nothing. They lived in a bad part of town and worked hard just to make ends meet.

Hearing the story of this family made me feel both grateful for my own blessings and inspired to give everything I could.

Beth gave me a list of the items the family needed, and my family got to work. As we ticked off items from the list, such as Bibles, gas cards, and coats, we became aware of just how needy this family was. It was so sad to see that the bare essentials were things that the kids wanted most. I explained to my family that we had "adopted" another family for Christmas, and so our family's Christmas might not be as full of gifts as years past. They were thrilled, and we shopped for the family's gifts together. On Christmas Day, we delivered their gifts as a family. It was so good for my kids to see how much this other family appreciated the things that we took for granted. It was the best lesson I could have taught my children and the best Christmas gift of all to my own family.

In this situation, I had to get creative to find a way to make a difference by giving. But it can also be very simple and easy to give to others. Here is a list of ways that you can help others so that you can get going—and get giving.

- Help an unemployed friend by offering to network him or her with some of your connections.

- Provide a letter of reference for a friend looking for a job.

- Give a compliment to someone at work who has performed well.

- Help your colleagues out by telling their boss how valuable they are to you and the company.

- Nominate one of your colleagues for an award at work.

- Become a mentor or coach to someone in need.

- Put your skills to use by participating in a nonprofit board or helping young men and women at organizations such as the YWCA and YMCA.

- Give your people time off to help recognize hard work.

- Offer to take on additional work in the office to help your boss or someone else look good.

- Write a simple letter to your associates who are performing well.

- Tell the people you love how much they mean to you and thank them for being an important part of your life.

- Give a complete stranger a compliment.

- In rush-hour traffic, let people cut over to your lane.

- Look people in the eyes, smile, and say hello.

- Offer babysitting services to friends who have small kids.

- Cook a meal for a friend, for no reason.

- Send a card or email to your friends and let them know you are thinking about them.

- Listen and let your friends vent their problems to you.

- Send a note of encouragement to a friend who is struggling.

- Give your boss a compliment.

- Help a friend financially, even if it's just a few dollars.

- Use your skills to do a friend a favor. For example, if you are a hairdresser, give friends in need a free haircut.

- Reach out and touch someone. Just your outstretched hand provides a connection.

- Ask, what can I do to help?

- Surprise your neighbor and cut his or her grass.

- Show that you genuinely care when people are in need.

- Go shopping or help run errands for an elderly neighbor.

- Buy a plane ticket for a friend to come visit you for a fun "getaway."

- Send flowers or cookies.

- Feed the homeless.

- Adopt a family.

- Be a Big Brother or Big Sister.

- Volunteer at a hospital or nursing home.

- Invite someone who you think is lonely to your home for dinner.

- Give an extra tip to a great server at a restaurant.

- Write a note to your maid in the hotel and tell her what a great job she did with a small tip.

- Go out of your way to compliment your co-workers—even to their managers.

- Let someone in front of you in line at the grocery store.

- Offer to walk your neighbor's dog.

- Make a donation to your church or temple.

- Bring lunch for a co-worker.

- Pay the bus fare for the person behind you.

- Hold the door for a stranger.

- Volunteer for a day at an animal shelter.

- Pick up litter that you see on the street.

- Thank your mail carrier.

- Tell your family you love them.

- Wash your neighbor's car.

- Drop off warm winter clothes at a Goodwill or homeless shelter.

HAPPINESS P.S.

There are many ways to help people. You will find those ways by reflecting on your own gifts and what you have to offer. When you do, you will notice the feeling that you get will be better than winning the lottery. I hope my stories in this chapter have inspired you to reach out and help someone.

:)

OH, HAPPY DAY: GET YOUR HAPPINESS ON THE CALENDAR NOW!

I'd like to start this chapter out with a few questions for you:

* How often do you check your planner?

* What are the most common items listed on your calendar?

* After glancing at your schedule, do you feel better or worse?

* How many personal events appear on your calendar?

* How many professional items appear on your calendar?

* How many items on your calendar reflect your state of happiness?

How is it possible that we spend so much time and energy in maintaining our schedules, and yet we so rarely book anything positive for ourselves? It's time to change the way we look at our schedules.

HAPPINESS NOTE CARD: MAKE HAPPINESS A PRIORITY

These days, it seems as though everyone you meet has an overflowing schedule. We can hardly find the time in our schedules for work, let alone for some "me time." However, when you really think about it, what is more important that becoming a happier person? When you become happier, you'll be a better friend, employee, parent, and person. So find time today to schedule some happiness on your calendar.

In this chapter, you'll learn how booking a little happiness and "me time" can change the way you approach your day, week, and even month. You'll also learn how overscheduling, whether at work, with friends, or at home, is detrimental for everyone involved. Finding a balance is tough, but it's a crucial step in your journey toward happiness.

SCHEDULE YOUR HAPPINESS

That's right, I said schedule it.

I don't know about you, but just about everything I do at work is on my schedule. If I don't have it written down in my Franklin planner, I will forget to do it. There have actually been times that I have left my Franklin planner at home and had to call my kids to have them read me my "to-dos" for the day! It's sad, but it's true. However, what you will find on my schedule are not only my work "to-dos" but my social "to-dos" and my family calendar. I literally write down whom I need to send encouraging cards to, whom I need to call, a long-lost friend I need to schedule time with. These are all on my calendar. Why? Because they are important to me. Seeing them there every day reminds me that my life is full not only at work but outside of work, and that time is worthy of scheduling as well. Because guess what? It's just as important as those critical work meetings or tasks that need to get done and, for me, it's more important. So pick up a pen, sharpen your time management skills, and get to it. Start blocking off time for those things that make you happy.

The other day, a very good friend of mine was talking to me about her upcoming fiftieth birthday. She was upset because she couldn't decide what she wanted to do to celebrate this monumental milestone. As we got to talking, I realized that the birthday planning wasn't really what was bothering her; she just wasn't in a good place in general. She was feeling depressed about turning fifty, struggling with her weight, and feeling lonely. She had gotten into the habit of complaining about being in a funk, often saying things like, "I just need to get out and laugh for a change." But instead of doing something to make herself feel better, she would just sit in her apartment, watch TV, eat bad food, and slip deeper into her lonely world.

I don't think she was ever consciously isolating herself or purposefully remaining unhappy, but it seemed like she wasn't motivated to change her routine of unhappy and unfulfilling behavior. From the outside looking in, I started to feel a little hopeless. "How can I help my friend?" I wondered. She had been a big part of my family for the past twenty years, but I knew I couldn't force her to become happy.

I wasn't too surprised that she was feeling uneasy about her upcoming birthday celebration. Lots of people feel uncomfortable about planning their own parties, and I figured she just wanted one of her friends to take over. I was, of course, thrilled to volunteer to help; there is nothing more satisfying than getting friends together to celebrate someone we all love and cherish. Then it dawned on me. She wasn't just uncomfortable with planning her birthday party. She was uncomfortable with planning anything that had to do with her own happiness. This was the reason she had been so lonely and unhappy lately.

I decided to challenge her on this. "First," I told her, "I'd love to help with your birthday." Her facial expression immediately told me that this was exactly what she was looking for. Of course, I was happy to help. But it was also time to address the second part of the situation: her loneliness. I said to her, "You know, you sit in your apartment far too much. That in itself will make you depressed. Why do you do that?" She shrugged her shoulders, and it looked as if she was going to cry. I carefully continued, "If you want to enjoy life, you have to make some investments in helping yourself. Happiness just doesn't come your way without any effort. Sometimes you even need to plan for your own happiness."

Of course, some happiness is spontaneous. We can't plan for our friends to call us with a funny story or for our co-workers to tell us hilarious jokes. But this doesn't mean that happiness is something that just pops up on its own. The reality is that we can set ourselves up for happiness in some very simple ways.

In my friend's case, I could see that she was unhappy because she felt lonely. She felt disconnected from her friends and interpreted the fact that they weren't calling as evidence that they weren't interested in being her friends anymore. This was absolutely not the case, but it took some convincing for her to believe me. I told her, "Listen. Everyone gets busy. Everyone has his or her own life, and sometimes you need to be the one to reach out first. This takes effort, for sure, but once you start planning and enjoying the plans you do make, you will soon realize how something as small as a simple phone or email invitation can turn your life around. Create a social calendar for yourself, and start reaching out to your friends. Just because they don't call you doesn't mean they don't want to hang out with you."

And do you know what happened? After my friend started making plans with her friends, things started to look up. Not only did she enjoy spending time with her friends and catching up on the things she'd missed, but she also found herself looking forward to her plans, which improved the quality of her work week. As soon as she started spending time with her friends, she realized how silly she had been to think that they weren't interested in her friendship. They'd just gotten busy and distracted, and they were thrilled to have her back in their lives. This realization even affected her work. She was much happier around the office and even started to socialize with folks at work she typically hadn't interacted with. These colleagues started to get involved in her work, helping her, and giving her advice. This made her time at work more enjoyable and even more productive.

Even though my friend was uncomfortable about reaching out and a little insecure about why she'd ended up as unhappy as she was, the effort she put into planning her happiness paid off—big time!

Now let's talk about your plans. Our first exercise will involve brainstorming ways you can plan for your own happiness. Then you've got to actually do them! It might be hard to take the first step, but remember how much happier my friend was after she became proactive about her happiness.

EXERCISE: YOU HAVE AN APPOINTMENT FOR HAPPINESS

To get started with this exercise, let me help you with a few examples of my own. Here is a short list of happy-making activities I can get on my calendar:

- Attend a networking event where I can meet new people
- Arrange a lunch for a new employee to welcome her to my company
- Write a "job well done" note to a direct report who has been working extra hard
- Ask my colleagues to go out for lunch or happy hour
- Find people at work who match my personality and get to know them
- Have a date night with my husband
- Send a note to a friend asking her to join me for a great dinner
- Bring dessert over to a friend's house, and catch up at the kitchen table over a cup of coffee
- Schedule a day at the spa
- Spend an hour catching up with old friends, whether by Facebook, LinkedIn, email, or written notes
- Plan to spend an hour reading a favorite book
- Schedule time to do a good deed
- Schedule time with new colleagues at work to get to know them better (you would be surprised how building those relationships can help you in many different ways)
- Schedule "mommy and me" dates with my kids, one at a time

• Budget an hour a week for doing yoga, taking walks, or riding my bike

Now it's your turn. What events make you happy? Do some research. Maybe one of your favorite groups is coming to town, and you can catch them in concert. Perhaps your favorite team will be playing in your area soon. Make a weekend out of it. The more you do the things you love, the happier you will be. And remember, you don't have to plan anything that will cost money. Often the most rewarding activities we do are absolutely free.

The following activities make me happy:

_____

_____

_____

_____

_____

The second part of this exercise is the most important. You've got to pick two or three items on your list and put them in your planner. You'll find yourself looking forward to how much you'll enjoy them, and then when you're done, you can mark each activity off with a smile on your face!

HELPING WORKAHOLICS FIND HAPPINESS

The more you make time for activities you enjoy, the happier you will be. Sometimes the biggest challenge is time, especially for those of you who are workaholics. When do you make time to be happy? Is all the extra time you put in at the office paying off? Is it making you happy? These can be pretty tricky questions to answer. You could say that you received a larger bonus or even got a promotion. So what? Is that how you define your happiness? If you are a big corporate executive with a big salary, does that define who you are? Does your family care what position you have? Does it really add to your happiness?

Let me ask you a few fairly intense questions to get you thinking about how you approach your job, your time at work, and your approach to your own happiness. You'll notice that I'm not asking you to write down your answers to these questions, because I know that these can be hard realizations to achieve, let alone to put down on paper. So give yourself the chance to honestly reflect on these questions:

DID YOU KNOW?

You'll perform better if you come to work with a fresh, rested, and happy mind than if you constantly stay in "work mode." I believe that most mistakes, most arguments, and most terminations are due to overwork and imbalance. Employees who enjoy their personal lives tend to be more engaged with their tasks and have much higher productivity with better results than those who feel compelled to work constantly. Employees who pursue happiness outside of work are also better at building relationships with colleagues, which makes them more likely to be promoted.

- Does work define who you are? When you meet new people, do you always include your job title in your introduction?

- At the end of your life, will you say, "I wish I'd worked more" or "I wish I'd spent more time with the ones I love"?

- What would your family say about the things that make you happy?

- How many special events with your family do you miss because of work?

- How often do you find time to maintain your friendships?

- When you are dead, who will mourn you, your company or your family?

- What will they say in your eulogy?

- Whom do you know more about, your family or your co-workers?

Yeah, these are heavy questions. However, I'm asking them because I hope they will help you reflect on the way you prioritize your life. We live in a work-obsessed, corporate-ladder culture, and it can be next to impossible to step back and really see our lives. Most of the executives who have coached me have learned far too late that they gave their hearts and souls to their jobs, rather than to the people they loved. This is a hard-learned lesson, and so I hope that you will be able to learn it sooner, not later.

If you are a workaholic, I am not trying to make you feel bad, but hopefully to help you realize there is a better life out there for you and your family. Trust me, I know work can be all-consuming. I know that it makes you feel good when you reap the rewards of hard work. I know how great it feels to get that promotion or award. I know the elation you feel when you get that end-of-year bonus. But I also know that adrenaline rush is like a dangerous drug that you can become addicted to. And I've seen too many people chase that professional high while their kids grow up without them.

So, to lighten things up a bit, let's think about how you can achieve both a happier personal life and a more balanced career. When you learn to balance the time and effort you spend at work with your personal life, not only will you achieve more happiness, but you'll also perform better at work. Didn't expect to hear that, did you? If you work all the time and don't feel you can break away for your own sanity and happiness, your company is really not getting the best of you. Most important, though, is the fact that workaholics are not actually the most likely to succeed professionally because they tend to be stressed, grouchy, and overwhelmed. And who wants to promote someone like that?

In addition to benefiting your career, learning to balance your personal and professional life will benefit your family and friends. They'll notice a huge difference in the way you interact with them when your life is in balance. And you'll enjoy the time you spend together more, since you won't be stressing about a project at work.

You may have to start out small by scheduling one event a week that makes you happy. Refer back to the lists you created on page 172. Happiness just doesn't come overnight; sometimes you have to work on it. But the good news is that working on your happiness is an enjoyable project.

This next story will demonstrate how your life can look if you don't schedule happiness and you are a workaholic. This is a true story about a person in my life to whom I've actually dedicated this chapter, Anne. She is a workaholic and needs more than ever to schedule time for happiness.

Anne is my mentor, colleague, and friend. She is amazing; she is smart, beautiful, and kind, and seems to have it all. But she's got one downfall: she is a workaholic. Anne has given the last thirty years of her life to her company; she works at least sixty hours a week every week. She always puts her direct reports above herself when scheduling time off. In fact, she often skips her own vacations because she's given away so much time to her employees. After spending so much time on her career, Anne noticed her college friends starting to fade away. Now she spends most of her time with colleagues. In a way, she has traded in her life for her career. Even though she's earned success, prestige, and power with her job, she often finds herself wondering if things could be different.

Anne has been a master at making time for productivity. She could work until 7:00 p.m. every day, babysit her step-daughter's kids, make a nice dinner, and still squeeze in a Pilates class. However, I guarantee if you asked her if she makes the time for happiness in her life, her answer would undoubtedly be "No way!" The only people who seem to be concerned about her happiness are her close friends. She needs to care about her happiness. And she needs to do something about it. Her company certainly isn't going to ask her to take time off to visit the spa or take a long lunch with girlfriends.

But Anne's situation can change—today. All it will take is for her to schedule a little happiness into her busy calendar. And if she can make time for a last-minute board meeting, she can make time for this, too.

Another example is my friend who is a vice-president with a hospitality company. Debra has spent the majority of her professional years working for this company, a company that has treated her well and that she loves. Debra never had children and always felt compelled to work additional hours in order to move ahead. Most of the time she worked sixty to eighty hours a week, never complaining but also always feeling that it was necessary. Then she got divorced because of all the time she spent at work. After the divorce, she reflected on her life and realized she had never really focused much on herself, let alone on her marriage. She started asking herself if all the time she spent at work was worth losing her marriage. The answer was undoubtedly no.

So she planned. She decided to start leaving work on time (or at a reasonable time) in order to rekindle the relationships she had lost and also to find a new companion. Her boss noticed that she was out of the office by 6:00 and no longer worked on weekends. In her review a few months later, he brought it up. Much to her surprise, instead of criticizing her, he praised her. Her boss explained he had always worried that work was too much a part of her life, that it was a negative driving force of her life. When she started taking time out for herself, she became a much better leader because she was happier and more engaged. She was providing a much better example as a leader in the company's goal of instilling a culture that supported a healthy work/life balance.

TOO FAR IN THE OTHER DIRECTION: CAN YOU BE TOO SOCIAL?

It's easy to see how you can miss out on happiness by overworking or overscheduling your family. But there is another way you might be missing out on happiness that might sound a little surprising. Did you know you can actually be too social? It might seem as though the people who spend every single night at fabulous party after fabulous party are the happiest people on earth, but it's not true.

A friend of mine is one of the busiest people I know. But she's not spending all of her time glued to her laptop or shuttling around kids. Instead, she's spending all of her time at different parties. She works in an industry in which socializing with vendors and sponsors is extremely important, so on any given night, she's hopping in and out of taxis, schmoozing this person and that. While it seems like a glamorous life, it robs her of the chance to ever spend any quality time by herself. She never gets the chance to relax, and so she never truly enjoys the events she attends. And when her friends invite her to a nice dinner party or brunch, she's too exhausted to go.

By penciling in one night a week to stay home and read a book or catch up on laundry while listening to music, my friend has rediscovered her happiness. Sure, it was hard at first to turn down a fabulous event full of celebrities and gift bags, but the resulting happiness was worth it. She can now enjoy the events she attends, spend time with her friends when she wants to, and even get some sleep.

FREEING UP TIME TO BE HAPPY

As part of this chapter and your next exercise, let's think about how we can start your calendar of happiness and arrange it according to your life. We talked about a few different scenarios that may hold you back when it comes to scheduling happiness, but it's time to get over that and start planning.

The first thing you should do is determine what obstacles are stopping you from actually scheduling happiness. Are you working too much? Spending too much time running your kids around? Are you spending too much time out on the town? Be honest! What's filling up too much of your calendar?

List the things that make scheduling happiness difficult for you below:

_____

_____

_____

_____

_____

If you're looking at your list and wondering how in the world you're going to find time for happiness, don't worry. Some things are easier to rearrange than others. Just try to tackle one item at a time to free up at least one night or a couple of afternoon hours a week.

B HAPPY 2DAY: USING TODAY'S TECHNOLOGY TO MAKE HAPPINESS A PRIORITY

Well, now that we've done some serious brainstorming about what makes us happy and what stands in the way of our happiness, it's time to take the next step and use technology to work some happiness into our schedules. While technology can often be a big pain in the backside, it can also be a fast and easy way to find happiness.

First and foremost, reaching out to old friends is a great way to bring happiness back into your life. So why not take advantage of the many social networking sites like LinkedIn, Twitter, MySpace, and Facebook? My mother-in-law is in her seventies and spends a good part of her morning catching up with her kids, grandkids, and friends. There is no age limit to this technology. Sign up and reach out to friends you haven't seen in years. Look up your old college roommate. Find your old neighbor. You'll be surprised at how easy it is to reconnect with friends.

The second thing you can do is create a "happiness calendar" online or using Microsoft Word. Fill this calendar in with the events you plan, and put it up somewhere you'll see it every day. Each time you pass the calendar, you can remind yourself of how much fun you'll have when you meet up with your friends, or just thank yourself for making your happiness a priority.

The third way to utilize technology in your quest for happiness is email. I don't know what I did before email—or texting for that matter! It has made my life so much easier. It has made connecting with friends, making new friends, and keeping up with old colleagues a breeze. It only takes five minutes to write a note to an old friend or schedule a date with a new friend. It breaks down barriers of anxiety about reaching out first or making up with someone you had an argument with. When you use your email to get in touch with friends instead of just for work, you'll actually look forward to opening your inbox.

Finally, use the Internet to help you increase your happiness. Look online at your local chamber of commerce, Facebook, or Craigslist for groups of people who have recently moved to your area and are looking for new friends. Or search the Internet for local book clubs or volunteer organizations.

Now that you know how beneficial scheduling happiness can be, don't waste any time. Soon you'll be able to look back over the questions at the beginning of this chapter and give very different answers. I hope this chapter helps you turn your calendar into something that cheers you up (rather than stresses you out).

HAPPINESS P.S.

Take the next month to reflect upon what you just read and wrote down about what you need to schedule. Find time to schedule at least one thing a week that will bring happiness into your life. At the end of the month, see how it made you feel. Try to increase the events to twice a week or as many times as you can make time for. You won't believe the difference it will make.

HAPPINESS TIP #9

WHEN ALL ELSE FAILS, JUST LAUGH

I was at a learning conference when a publisher approached me about writing a book. My first response was "Heck no! I've got nothing else to write about learning that hasn't been written before!" You see, I'd already contributed to four books on learning. The publisher laughed and said, "No, I want you to write a book on happiness. You have a following at these conferences, and it's because of the positive energy you exude." "Oh," I thought. "Now that I could do."

HAPPINESS NOTE CARD: IS LAUGHTER REALLY THE BEST MEDICINE?

While researchers aren't sure if the actual act of laughing is what makes people feel better, there is little doubt that people who have a good sense of humor feel better than those who don't.

In fact, some hospitals even have "laughter rooms," where patients can check out funny movies or see a clown do funny tricks. Some "laughter rooms" even host comedians who come in and entertain the patients for hours. People who attend these laughter rooms on a regular basis recover from their illnesses faster and even require less pain medication. Wow.

The reason I felt that I confident I could write a book on happiness isn't because I've lived a perfectly happy life—far from it! What I have lived is a philosophy that you can cultivate a strong sense of happiness, regardless of what you're going through. I understand, maybe better than most, that sometimes life just gives you lemons. I believe that it's how you handle your situation, your circumstances, and your day-to-day life that makes the difference. This is what I mean by being powered by happy. It's when you make the choice every single day to stoke your brain with positive thoughts, laughter, gratitude, forgiveness, kindness, and recognition. And this is why I felt that writing this book was something I could do.

In earlier chapters, I talked about strategies for finding and maintaining happiness in a variety of situations. But there is one thing we haven't discussed that can be the fastest and easiest way to find little moments of happiness and give you the boost of endorphins you need to get through the day: laughter. I laugh every single day. Sometimes it's a big belly laugh that stays with me for hours and hours, and sometimes it's just a quiet chuckle I let out when I read a funny joke or see a cute picture. By laughing every day and as often as I can, I've made it a habit. People see me laughing, and they want to laugh. It's like a form of contagious happiness.

In this chapter, you'll learn the benefits of laughter as well as find a list of great ways to bring laughter back into your life. Making laughter a part of your day-to-day life will make you—and everyone around you—happier.

Why laugh? Laughing is a simple act we all know how to perform (even if we're a little rusty!). If you need any motivation for a good laugh, look no further: Eric Chudler, a neuroscientist at the University of Washington, lists the following benefits of laughing:

- Relieving muscle tension

- Reducing your blood pressure

- Increasing your heart rate

- Helping to oxygenate your blood by changing your breathing

- Boosting your immune system

IT'S OKAY TO CHUCKLE ALONE

If you haven't laughed for a while, it may take a little practice to bring a healthy dose of laughter back into your routine. But don't worry—it's a project you'll love working on.

The first misconception about laughter, I believe, is that it's something that only happens when you're out with others. Who says you can't laugh when you're alone? I find a good giggle fit when I'm by myself to be as satisfying and rejuvenating as a massage. I often find myself chuckling at a funny thought when I'm walking down the street—and I seem to be especially vulnerable to funny thoughts when I'm in an elevator with a stranger. But once they see that I'm just laughing at a private thought, ten times out of ten, they start smiling or even laughing with me. It's contagious!

Here are some great ways to get laughing by yourself:

- Read a funny book.
- Watch a funny movie or TV show.
- Watch an old home video or look through an old photo album. Go ahead, laugh at that old hairstyle!
- Listen to a funny podcast while you're doing chores or running errands.
- Read the comics in the newspaper.
- Write funny postcards to your friends—and send them. Think of how much they'll laugh when they get them.
- Turn on the radio and belt out the tunes.

LAUGHING WITH YOUR FAMILY

Laughing alone is great, but why not share the joy? When we laugh, we encourage others to laugh. And then everyone can enjoy the benefits of laughter. Try to make it a routine to laugh at least once with your family each day. If you have kids, encourage them to tell jokes at the dinner table. Watch a funny movie together. Play a board game.

Laughing with your family can help you forget about a stressful day, form bonds with your children or spouse, and just feel better.

Here is a list of great activities to get your family laughing together:

- Play charades.

- Go to a family-friendly comedy club together.

- Do a scavenger hunt around the house.

- Sing karaoke to your favorite songs.

- Play Pictionary.

- Invent new personas, and try them out at a restaurant or on a walk.

- Have a knock-knock joke contest.

- Play dress-up.

So give it a shot! Brainstorm seven things you can do this week with your family that will get them all laughing:

1. _____

_____

_____

_____

2. _____
   _____
   _____
   _____

3. _____
   _____
   _____
   _____

4. _____
   _____
   _____
   _____

5. _____
   _____
   _____
   _____

6. _____
   _____
   _____
   _____

7. _____

_____

_____

_____

LAUGH WITH YOUR CO-WORKERS

Your office might not be the first place that comes to mind when you think of comedy, but that doesn't mean it can't be a great place to laugh. Laughing at work can help you get to know your co-workers, ease tension during teamwork, and relieve stress when you're working on tight deadlines. Who said we can't have fun at work?

While your boss might not want you to work on your stand-up routine on the clock, you can still insert some humor into your corporate life. Instead of initiating conversations with your co-worker about how stressed you are, tell a funny story about your morning—and laugh. You'll be surprised at how quickly your co-worker will laugh with you, and how it can help start powerful relationships in the workplace. Start meetings by asking if anyone has a good (and appropriate) joke. This can set the tone for an open and productive meeting.

If you cultivate an easy laugh and do your best to spread it around your office, you will be not only a happier person but also a more sought-after co-worker. If you're consistently good-natured and quick to laugh, people will enjoy working with you and you'll get more opportunities for growth. See? Laughter really is a great thing.

I have found that networking and other professional relationships are in many cases built on laughter. Many of the stories that you will read in this chapter—while silly and perhaps seemingly inappropriate for the workplace—have opened doors for me as a corporate trainer, in tense networking situations, and in building valuable business relationships with colleagues who have turned into friends. We work too hard and too long to not find humor somewhere in the forty to sixty hours a week we spend at the office.

When people laugh, it helps bring a smile to others and helps create a fun, open culture. When associates feel comfortable enough to laugh openly and share a few funny stories, they are engaged in the workplace. A work environment where your associates are engaged is the best work environment there is. And trust me, it's much better to be around people at work who enjoy laughter as much as you do, than people who don't.

TURNING AN EMBARRASSING MOMENT AROUND

Some things in life are easy to laugh at. It's easy to laugh at a funny movie or a well-timed joke. But it's not always easy to laugh at yourself—especially when you've just done something unbelievably embarrassing. However, I've learned that having a sense of humor can turn a mortifying event into a productive moment. Embarrassing moments can be the best way to make new friends, strengthen existing relationships, and learn about yourself. Let's face it, we all embarrass ourselves every now and then. Since we can't avoid the occasional slipup, we may as well learn to make the best of them. My life has been built upon these types of embarrassing moments.

Full Moon at Thirty Thousand Feet

My husband is notoriously hard to impress when it comes to receiving gifts. He appreciates the thought and effort that the gift giver put into his present, but he just doesn't do much to show it. So shortly after we were married, I decided to surprise him with a really great gift. Little did I know I'd also set myself up for one of the most embarrassing moments of my life.

I bought my husband tickets to a North Carolina State vs. North Carolina basketball game, which required us to fly to where it was being played. We'd only flown a few times before, so this was an extremely exciting part of the gift. (And yes, I did get a slightly more enthusiastic response from my husband when he opened his gift. I believe it was something along the lines of "Oh, cool!")

Shortly after the plane took off, I got up to use the restroom. While I waited for the little "vacant" sign to pop up on the accordion door, I chatted with the three men who were unfortunately seated about six inches from the restroom.

Once it was finally my turn, I stepped into the little bathroom and did my business. As I stood up with my pants around my ankles, I saw a sign telling me not to flush any objects down the toilet. I turned around and saw another one—and another! "Does toilet paper count as an object?" I wondered. "What if I flushed the toilet paper and it did something to the plane's engine? What if my careless flush brought the whole plane down?!" But after a while, I figured that I didn't really have any alternative. I flushed the toilet paper and turned around to pull my pants up. And then I realized that the accordion door was wide open. I stood up, horrified, and saw that the three men I'd been chatting with earlier had had front row seats to my whole to-flush-or-not-to-flush dilemma.

Mortified, I screamed and slammed the door, locking myself in the little bathroom. As I stared at myself in the cloudy little bathroom mirror, I contemplated hiding until the plane landed, but figured that the flight attendants would probably force me out before that could happen. So, knowing that I had no alternative, I decided to find a way to see something positive about my situation before braving the aisle. As a new flier, I thought that at least I'd learned a very valuable lesson: locking the bathroom door is vitally important for any visits to the aerial commode. I'd also probably just embarrassed myself more fully than I could have imagined, so at least I'll never do anything more embarrassing (on a flight, that is!). And, I thought, I will be able to give my husband another great gift—the laugh of his lifetime! So I squared my shoulders, hurried back to my seat, and told my husband a story that still absolutely cracks him up.

Look Out, Charlie!

After I had my first daughter, I assumed that I needed to get a minivan. I shopped around for a bit and found one and that was truly huge. It was a mini conversion van (with curtains, thank you very much!). I practically had to sit on a phone book to see over the steering wheel. It certainly wasn't fit for my five-foot-one stature, and I would soon learn that it wasn't the best for my visibility either.

One day I was on my way to work and running late for a managers' meeting. As I rushed out of my neighborhood, I looked down to see the gas light illuminated. "Crap!" I thought to myself. "I have to get gas!" I pulled into the gas station as fast as I could, jumped out of my van, and started to pump the gas. As I tapped my foot, urging the gas to hurry up, I saw a sign that read, "We only accept CASH or a BP card." Again, crap! I had neither. So I stopped pumping right around three dollars and ran into the gas station, where two older men stood staring at me from behind the counter. Out of breath, I said, "I am so sorry, but I just pumped three dollars' worth of gas and do not have either cash or a BP credit card. Can I leave my driver's license with you to prove I will come back and pay you?" The old men had clearly never dealt with a situation like this. As one scratched his head, he said, "Well, Charlie, what are we going to do?" Charlie's response was, "I reckon we should let her go but keep her license, just like she said." "Awesome!" I screamed. "I will be back around five!"

I thought to myself, "My day is turning around!" I jumped in my van, threw on my seat belt, and took off. But wait! The entire van jerked back and forth as though I had just run over something very big! Crap! Did I run over Charlie?

Almost scared to open my door, I jumped down from my seat, only to see the cashier running toward me, screaming with his hands above his head. It sounded like he was yelling for Charlie to shut off the gas, but I couldn't quite tell. Relieved that it wasn't Charlie that I ran over, I looked to my left in time to see a volcano of gas erupting from the gas pump. Not just from the pump (because that, clearly, was still stuck in my van) but out of the container that the gas comes out of. I had torn the hand pump (and entire container) from its stand. I looked down in panic. My black velvet pumps were swimming in gas. My God, it was a river. I have never seen so much gas. After Charlie shut off the gas and the volcano stopped erupting, I quietly asked, "You guys have insurance, right?"

Somehow I still managed to make it to my morning meeting that day, though my shoes stunk like gas and I am sure I looked a little frazzled. When my boss called building maintenance to come and check out the gas leak (many people in the office had apparently become concerned about the smell of gas), I was forced to come clean. After I told him about my morning incident, he laughed and told me he was glad I was so enthusiastic about being on time. He had no idea!

First Position, Second Position, Run!

A writer I know once learned a valuable lesson during an excruciatingly embarrassing moment. She had been living in Rome, Italy, for a few months when she decided to enroll in a ballet class so that she could improve her Italian and meet some new friends. She hadn't taken ballet since she was a six-year-old, so she figured that a beginner's class would be the perfect fit.

As she changed in the tiny locker room for her first class, she realized that she might have misunderstood the class description. All around her, Italian women were stepping into leotards with brightly colored tights and fashionable leg warmers. "Maybe it's just an Italian fashion thing?" she wondered as she pulled on her baggy sweat pants and hooded sweatshirt.

Only when the teacher began shouting instructions in rapid-fire Italian did my friend realize how out of her league she really was. All around her, ballerinas struck pose after graceful pose, pirouetting and leaping as if they had spent their entire lives working on achieving perfect form. After an agonizing hour, during which my friend sweated and grunted her way through each awkward position, the teacher announced something that, as best as my friend could understand, translated into "freestyle time."

"Thank God," she thought, "I can finally get a break." Boy, was she wrong! All of her classmates formed a large circle as the teacher put a techno CD into the stereo. To my friend's horror, one by one, ballerinas pranced into the center of the circle to perform their best routines for their classmates. Women were leaping, spinning, and kicking to the music like pros. When it came to my friend's turn, she shook her head quickly, mumbling that she didn't want to do a solo routine. The teacher scoffed something in rushed Italian and nudged my friend into the center of the circle, where she stood, frozen. After a few measures of techno music, my friend thought, "Well, might as well give it a shot!" and started dancing. Sure, she had absolutely zero idea of what she was doing or how it looked, but as she got going, she started to have fun! She tried a couple of twirls (and lost her balance a few times) and even did a couple of leaps. When she finally left the center of the circle, laughing, her classmates burst into applause! They knew that she was completely unprepared for being put on the spot, and they loved that she tried it.

Even though my friend was mortified about having to dance in the center of a ring of professional ballerinas, she gave it a shot. And by putting herself out there, she made some of her best friends in Italy in that studio. Sure, she was known as "that silly American," but she didn't care.

It's a Bird. It's a Plane. It's a...Bug?

A few years ago, I was lucky enough to be invited to a user-group meeting by one of my vendors. It was held at a beautiful bed-and-breakfast overlooking a scenic golf course and country club. We were wined and dined, and it was an honor to have been invited. Over the four-day retreat, the other meeting participants and I were treated like VIPs while we learned all about the vendor's business.

On the last day, the vendor's CEO had planned an elaborate and very formal meeting to discuss his future vision with us, his customers. We were all looking forward to his presentation and took our seats at a long conference table. I ended up sitting at the end of the table next to a woman named Vicky, whom I'd met at the beginning of the retreat. I could tell she was a great person, and I felt as though we could potentially become friends.

About halfway through the CEO's presentation, I noticed something large and black on the wall behind him. I didn't want to squint too hard at whatever it was and insult the CEO if he noticed my wandering eyes, but I couldn't take my eyes off of it. Was it some kind of electrical appliance? And then, to my horror, it moved. Was it a bird? A bat that had somehow wandered out during the day and was now trapped inside the building? Then, as if the creature could tell I was thinking about him, it left the wall and started to hover, directly behind the CEO. I started to panic, "What is this thing?!"

At this point, I could tell that Vicky and some of the other attendants were staring, transfixed at the gigantic mutant creature. It must be a bug, I realized—a giant, evil, diabolical bug, who seemed to be staring right...at...me. The CEO, meanwhile, hadn't noticed the monster hovering behind him and was surely starting to wonder what all of his customers were doing, staring blankly behind him. Then, before any of us could see it coming, the bug dive-bombed—and hit me! The meeting, which mere seconds ago had been completely composed and professional, turned into a scene from a war movie, with all the attendees hitting the deck. Even the CEO took cover! We never did learn exactly what type of dinosaur bug this was.

So there we were, under the conference room table, laughing hysterically at what had just transpired. Vicky and I might not have gotten the CEO's full pitch or learned everything he'd hoped we would, but we did become fast friends. Sometimes it takes an embarrassing moment for professionals to form a bond. By laughing at our silly fear of a bug (albeit a giant bug), we were able to relax a bit, let down our guards, and become real friends. And sometimes that's the most you can hope for.

EXERCISE: GETTING TO KNOW YOU...AND YOUR MOST EMBARRASSING MOMENTS

One of the best icebreakers that you can use for a team meeting or professional training is Two Truths and a Lie. In this game, the people in the room write down three things about themselves. Two are true; one is a lie. Everyone tries to figure out which one is the lie. It is a great way to get to know your colleagues and perhaps even new employees.

Another fun "getting-to-know-you" game—whether you are at work or at a party—is to go around the room and ask people to name their most embarrassing moments. This is a great exercise for getting people to talk because (a) everyone has embarrassed themselves at some point, and (b) laughing about those moments can bring everyone together. You will be surprised at how much you learn about each other and how hard you'll laugh.

Let's get ready by writing your most embarrassing moment. When you are done, try it out. Tell this story out loud to a friend, laugh, and see how it makes you (and your friend) feel!

_____

_____

_____

_____

_____

_____

_____

Whether you are at work or at home, laughing is good for your soul. To be happier at work, find ways to laugh. Find ways to make others laugh. Make it an environment where people want to go every day.

HAPPINESS P.S.

What can you do to laugh more at work? What can you do to make others laugh more?

Write down three things that you can do to make your culture a bit more fun every day. Learn to laugh. Challenge yourself and others to make this part of your every day.

_____

_____

_____

_____

:)

PACK UP YOUR HAPPINESS AND TAKE IT TO WORK

HOW CAN HAPPINESS REALLY HELP YOU AT WORK?

By now you've read my tips for how to find, maintain, and even power up the happiness you deserve in life. Much of the discussion in this book addresses your happiness at work for an important reason: No matter how long you've been working, what kind of work you do, or whom you work for, you spend a good part of your life at work. Outside of family, it's likely that your most frequent interactions with others happen at work. So your happiness (or, unfortunately, unhappiness) at work can color just about every aspect of your life. Think about the last time you had a terrible day at work. Undoubtedly, it robbed you of some of the happiness you might have enjoyed during the rest of that precious twenty-four-hour period of your life.

But the reality is, work is hard. Achieving happiness there 100 percent of the time can be challenging, if not impossible. A young associate I hired a few years ago, when she was barely out of college, enlightened me about what I believe is a generational difference in how people view work. She put it simply: "I work only so I can enjoy and be happy with the other parts of my life. And I want the work to be truly satisfying, not just something that yields a paycheck. If it's not, I'll look for something else." Wow, I thought, that's a pretty tall order! In contrast, my parents and grandparents viewed work as essential to the survival of their families. They did it to put food on the table, a table that during the Great Depression sometimes included a large extended family. Often, they found it necessary to forgo job satisfaction for job security.

No matter which point of view describes your motivations for working, work is a lot harder than it was thirty years ago. Companies are asking fewer employees to do more work. Layoffs have become commonplace, which adds to the stress. There are more financial pressures and intense global competition. Unless you're one of the lucky few, the challenges you can face at your job, no matter how ideal it seems, can create an all-out assault on your happiness.

That's why I have an entire chapter dedicated to how you can be one of those productive, successful, and respected employees whose workday is powered by happy.

> ### HAPPINESS NOTE CARD: WHEN THE GOING GETS TOUGH, THE TOUGH LOOK FOR ANOTHER JOB
>
> Because we spend so much time at work, there is no reason to put up with a negative work climate. Sometimes the best way to remedy a bad job culture is to leave it. Life is way too short to spend as many hours as you do at work being miserable. It will affect not only your future with the company (who wants a miserable co-worker, boss, or direct report?) but also your life with your family and friends. Are you willing to take that chance?

INSPIRING IDEAS FOR FINDING HAPPINESS AT WORK

I've often found that the best advice about increasing your happiness at work comes from those who live it every day. I asked some of the happiest people I've worked with over the last twenty-five years to share their tips.

* **Be the friend/co-worker that you would want others to be to you.** You might be surprised how much happiness is returned to you when you show yourself as a genuine, positive, and respected colleague.

* **It's an old cliché, but "assume innocence."** It really does work, and it eliminates a lot of conflict with others. Don't create those imaginary stories about what others may have done to you on purpose or are saying behind your back.

Assume that your colleagues are acting with the very best of intentions.

- **Work on developing great friends at work.** They can become lifelong allies, and they understand the daily pressures you may be feeling better than anyone else.

- **Be humble.** As someone once told me, "check your ego at the door."

- **If you're not happy in your current job, make a life change to something that you have always wanted to do.** (It's never too late!)

- **Always help other people, even when you don't feel like it.** It will give you a great feeling of satisfaction, and people will return the favor when you need it most.

- **You get out of your work what you put into it.** Be a team player. Pull your weight.

- **Keep complaining to a minimum.** We all need to vent, but find out whom you can vent to and then keep it to a dull roar.

- **Understand that work is a business.** If decisions are made that aren't what you would have done, understand that it isn't personal. Internalizing things over which you have no control can siphon off happiness faster than anything else.

- **Maintain your perspective.** Don't overreact. Think through all actions so that you don't live in regret.

- **Know that others are looking at you and emulating you.** Act in such a manner that someday one of your associates will tell you that you were instrumental in his or her career.

- **Love what you do.**

- **Leave it at work.**

- **Take time off and spend it with your family.**

- **Don't sweat the small stuff.**

- **Celebrate the little wins.**

- **Keep everything in perspective.**

- **Don't let bad days or bad events get you down.** You will always have another opportunity to make things better.

- **Try to be patient with others.** Even the best communicators can't always get their points across the first time around.

- **Sometimes you have to slow down and bring people along.** Going it alone is no fun in the long run.

- **Start and end your day with gratitude.** Use the time you spend walking in the door and out the door to think about what you're grateful for.

- **Praise and recognize the efforts of others**—and enjoy the responses you receive in return.

- **Get to know the people around you.** Find out their hidden talents. They can be great resources for you, and it's much easier to work with people when you care about them. Keep in mind that people generally don't care how much you know until they know how much you care.

- **Learn from your mistakes—we've all made them—just don't dwell on them.** Move on and try again.

- **Recognize others for a job well done.** It's contagious and it motivates everyone!

- **Make an effort to get to know the people you work with.** They can become a big part of your life; you might as well like them.

- **Be true to yourself.** If you are not happy, find out why and change what you can.

- **Make sure your personal values are aligned with the corporate values in the organization that employs you.**

- **Do what you are passionate about.**

- **Help others more than they help you.**

Isn't this great advice? Hopefully hearing from others who have found happiness at work will give you some ideas and thoughts to reflect on.

EXERCISE: CREATING HAPPY FOR OTHERS

Now let's reflect a bit on how you treat those around you. If you're a manager, try to answer these questions—and be honest! Remember, it's never too late to make a change.

- When was the last time you thanked your associates for the work they have done?

- When was the last time you recognized them on work well done?

- When was the last time you told your associates how valued they are with your organization?

- When was the last time you asked your associates if they are happy in their job and doing the work they want to do?

- When was the last time you asked your associates what you can do to help them move forward or develop them further?

- Are you happy at work? If not, how can you change it?

Now, after you reflected on these questions, do you feel that you can improve your culture or work environment, either for yourself or for the associates working for you? I want you to think of five things you can do better as a leader to impact the culture of your department, division, or even company. Sometimes it just takes one group or even one person to change the culture of an organization.

Some examples could include the following:

- Send personal notes to your associates to thank them for their hard work.

- Have a "recognition lunch" for your associates after a big project has been completed.

- Recognize a special person in front of your group or in front of the CEO.

- If you sit at the leadership table with the CEO, talk about the importance of culture within your organization. Tell him or her that taking care of your associates should be a top priority.

- Take a personal interest in your associates—get to know them!

- Ask your associates how they're doing periodically. Walk around and check on them.

- Reward people who work wisely and efficiently, rather than workaholics who contribute to a negative culture.

What can I do?

_____

_____

_____

_____

_____

LIFE IN CORPORATE AMERICA: IT CAN BE HARD ON HAPPINESS

As I described at the beginning of this chapter, we all know that work is not easy. Sometimes we have to temporarily become workaholics to meet the needs of our business or to do our job. However, it should be temporary, and when it becomes the norm rather than the exception, it's time to reevaluate.

I recently spoke at a conference on the topic of "women in leadership." It was a fabulous session, not because of my presentation but because of the audience of women who surrounded me. There was standing room only in my room, people sitting on the floor, and people outside the door. After the session was over, a woman actually said to me, "I felt like you were having a women's session in your living room. It was very comfortable, and I believe you helped many women today." That was the best review I have received to date for any of my conference or business speeches. Whether you are a woman or man, life in corporate work (or even public and nonprofit work) can be difficult. You need to vent; you need to talk through the challenges that you have in order to move beyond them and create a plan or solution to your challenges, even if it means leaving your job.

In this session, I had a bright young woman explain her situation and ask a profound question. She explained that she works in a culture where working overtime is valued and vital for promotions. She felt conflicted because she wanted to spend more time with her young children, but she also wanted to move up in her career. I asked her, "Who said you had to work lots of overtime to move ahead?" She replied, "It is the culture in which we work. All the executives work until 8:00 p.m. every night and highlight those associates who do the same." We talked about her performance and the fact that she is known as the speedy one, the unique one who gets her job done well with a high level of results against her goals. Wow! As a manager, I would be in heaven with an associate like that. I have seen dozens of my colleagues consistently work overtime because they are just plain inefficient or talk too much during work and can't get their job done in eight hours.

At the end, she asked me what I would do in her situation. I had one simple answer: leave. I told her, "You by yourself will not turn that culture around. It is like trying to turn around an elephant in a closet. Unless you want to work overtime, which you say you do not, you need to leave to get ahead. Many companies would love to have associates like you and be glad to offer you the promotion you deserve."

I recognized this woman's situation far too well. It's something I see all the time. People get sucked into work environments that don't fit their personalities or lifestyles and that are often dominated by poor management. This has taught me the importance of how leaders and culture are a critical part of evaluating a new company and job. People usually don't leave their company; they leave their boss. I knew that this woman could stay in her job, but if she did, her unhappiness at work would start to seep into her valuable time with her family.

This happened to me once. Not only was working

overtime expected, especially with my senior-vice-president title, but anyone who didn't put in enough overtime was publicly flogged! I was also expected to travel extensively for things that weren't critical, which robbed me of time with my family. This job was wrong for me in so many ways, but it took my daughter's intervention for me to figure it out. When Madison was in second grade, she started writing little letters that she would leave around the house for my husband and me to find. These notes were adorable, not only because of their misspellings and youthful honesty but also because they reminded me of why I was working in the first place: to give my kids a better life. And how could I do that if we were never together?

The first note wasn't addressed to anyone. It said, "Hi, I'm Madison. I would like to say is I love you even if you are my mom or my dad. If you are one of them, it is speshley for you. Circle Mom or Dad. If you are my mom, I would like to say I want to spend more time with you more. And if you are my dad, I would like to say is thank you and do you no why? Well here is why it is good. So you rally are home with me. No afense mom, I jest want you to get a knew job so you can spend time with all of us like me, dad, tiffany, or nieman. We all rally rally love you."

The second note was addressed to me. It said, "Mom, I love you so much and I don't want you to travel so much. I need u all the time. Your not there for me when your traveling.

When I was sick u got home and you took care of me you can't do that when your traveling for one week ever secent week. Love, Madison."

The third note was addressed to my boss. It said, "Dear John, I want to spend time with my mom more. I don't want my mom leveing me every secent week for one hole week. I never knew that she had to leave me that lng. I'm 8 years old and I still don't want her leveing me. Pleas don't let her leve me that long agen. I love her and when I'm sick I need her when know one is there for me I need my mom there for me. From Madison T."

A few months after I received these letters (and I wish I could have done it sooner), I resigned. I used the letters as part of my resignation. When my boss's boss came to me and tried to get me to stay, I simply let her read the letters and she understood. Luckily, I left on good terms. I just wish I would have left earlier and done a better job evaluating the company's culture before committing to the position. I am now part of an organization where work/life balance is the number one priority. I, and my family, have never been happier.

It's actually become a joke in our family about how much I am home now, how much time I do spend with my kids. Recently, I did have to travel to Pittsburgh to visit a client, and Madison said to me in the middle of a story, "Well, Mom, you weren't here for that. You were traveling." My older daughter, Tiffany, jumped up and yelled, "Madison, don't give Mom the guilt trip, or she will start being with us even more than she is now!"

I love it. I love the fact that I have turned my work around so my family knows they come first. Although I made lots of money and had a big title in my old job, none of that was worth the sadness I was bringing to my children. Thank God I made changes before it was too late.

CONCLUSION

HOW TO TAKE ALL THESE TIPS AND TRANSLATE THEM TO YOUR WORK LIFE

We now know that by becoming a happy person, you can have a much fuller life with your family, your friends, and your career.

And why is it so important to think about happiness and your career?

Recently I asked my daughter Tiffany, who is getting ready to start the next chapter in her life at college, if she felt that I was ever a "bad" mom for working. Did she ever feel like work came first? Was I the mom she needed and wanted? Her answer was, "You were and are the best mom and have always been a great example for me of how a woman can have it all. Because you were happy at work, you were happy with us at home." All the guilt from years past of being a working mom melted away. (P.S. I can't take ALL the credit; it helps when you have a supportive husband!)

Since I've given you a lot to think about in this book, I am going to summarize the chapters for you with key messages to consider as you start your journey toward a happier life at home and work.

HOT TIP #1: CREATE YOUR OWN DEFINITION OF HAPPINESS

We are all busy and running to make every minute count in our lives. However, how many of you have ever stopped to think about what happiness means to you? Reflecting on what makes you happy helps bring focus to what you are trying to achieve. Your happiness definition does not have to focus on one thing; it actually could be several parts, some for your home life and some for work. They are usually pretty different anyway. Understanding what happiness means to you is the first step in achieving it.

HOT TIP #2: CHOOSE HAPPINESS AND MAKE IT HAPPEN

My husband is often asked, "Is Beth always this happy?" His response is usually the same: "Yes. Annoyingly so!" As you have read throughout this book, I have had my own personal struggles in my life. However, happiness is all in how you cope with what you have been dealt. It is your attitude toward being happy and choosing to be happy that brings you through the tough times with a smile on your face. This goes for work, too: if you are not happy, make the decisions that will remedy this. It might be difficult or frightening, but you need to change the situation that is making you unhappy. Whether you find a new job within your company, deal with a bad boss, or leave altogether, it is more important to find happiness than to stick it out in a miserable situation. Staying in a bad work environment is just not worth sacrificing your happiness.

HOT TIP #3: AVOID WHAT HOLDS YOUR HAPPINESS HOSTAGE: MINIMIZING WORRY AND NEGATIVE THOUGHTS

We deal with lots of things that stand in the way of our happiness. Sometimes just reflecting on what is holding your happiness hostage will help you begin to overcome it. Collectively, we spend far too much time worrying about our problems, complaining about them, or simply avoiding them, when we could be confronting them and moving on. This is important to keep in mind as you go through your career. Issues that come up in the workplace can either dominate your time and stand in the way of your progress, or they can be dealt with quickly and efficiently. Separate fact from fiction. When confronted with a new worry or problem, don't let yourself get overwhelmed by the unknown, and absolutely don't let your mind run away from you. Learning to decipher what is causing the problem, what you can change, and what you cannot will save you weeks, months, and—heck—even years of unnecessary worry.

HOT TIP #4: HANG WITH A GANG THAT GETS IT

Who wants to hang with negative people? Being around negative people can not only affect your overall attitude toward happiness, but also how others see you. I tell my girls that when they hang out with the wrong kids at school, they can be seen as guilty by association. If they hang with the "mean girls," people who don't know them will consider them mean girls too. If you are hanging with people at work who are negative, then guess how you'll be perceived? On the other hand, how do you think being with a positive group can affect your life and happiness? You guessed it! Not only will you pick up on some of the happy vibes your friends exude, but you'll also be seen as a positive person by those who don't know you.

HOT TIP #5: DUMP THE TO-DO LIST AND START AN I-WISH LIST

We all have to-do lists, especially at work. They can get pretty overwhelming, so when your to-do list starts to get in the way of your happiness, take a quick peek at your wish list. Your to-do list might change daily or maybe even every hour, but your wish list will bring you back to your big-picture life goals. I have a lot of career goals that have been satisfied and some that have not, but I am still working on them—and they give me hope for my future! Looking at your wish list every once in a while can help you get perspective on your day-to-day stresses, and it can remind you of all the wonderful things you've got to look forward to.

HOT TIP #6: TAKE THE "UN" OUT OF "UNHAPPY" AND BE GRATEFUL

Unhappiness comes in many forms. Sometimes it comes from something out of our control, and sometimes it is self-inflicted. Often it is within our control to change from being unhappy to happy. We take for granted our family, our friends, and even our jobs. What would happen if we turned that around and, instead of thinking about all the things that are going wrong, we focused on the things that are going right? Being grateful brings a better attitude and helps us become aware of how blessed we really are.

HOT TIP #7: MAKE A HIGH-YIELD HAPPINESS INVESTMENT

One thing I have learned in my career is that helping those who are in need is an investment that pays off. The happiness that you get from helping others is more sustainable than winning the lottery. Knowing that you made a difference in someone's life will help you feel better as well as impact the way others feel about you. Senior leadership looks positively upon employees who are mentors and trusted colleagues. Soon you will find that by helping others without wanting to be noticed, you will be noticed in a big way by means of a promotion. Putting yourself in a leadership position helps your boss see you in a different light and proves to him or her that you are capable of great things. I have always told the people I mentor to behave as though they are one level higher, and soon they will find themselves being promoted, because they've already proven themselves capable of the job.

HOT TIP #8: OH, HAPPY DAY: GET YOUR HAPPINESS ON THE CALENDAR NOW!

We have no problem getting our work on the calendar. Meetings, deadlines, and project schedules fill our planners. However, your happiness is in jeopardy if that is the only scheduling you do. Use the same technology to schedule some happiness on your calendar. Start small. Schedule a lunch with a colleague or boss, and you'll kill two birds with one stone: you'll get out of the office for some fresh air and good food, and you'll build a working relationship with someone who can help you advance your career. Why wouldn't you do this? But don't only think of scheduling happiness at work. Mark your calendar with fun events with your family and friends. You'll be surprised at how much a little fun will pay off—at work and at home.

HOT TIP #9: WHEN ALL ELSE FAILS, JUST LAUGH

You now know more about me than you probably ever wanted to after reading this chapter. I think one of my gifts is that I don't take life (or my work) so seriously that I miss out on the funny side of life. Laughter is the best medicine. Just hearing people laugh brings a smile to my face. Think of the stories that you have, usually your most embarrassing moments, and share them with your friends. Trust me, it won't be long before you're laughing. When you are at work, this is important to remember. Laughing and having fun at work helps create a culture that is enjoyable to be a part of. On more than one occasion, I've had to leave meetings because of a case of the "giggles." Have I ever gotten in trouble for laughing? No way! People interpret my laughter as a sign of my good attitude and passion for life.

HOT TIP #10: PACK UP YOUR HAPPINESS AND TAKE IT TO WORK

We all spend way too much time at work to be miserable. We have talked about the importance of understanding what being happy at work means to you. What changes do you need to make in order to be happy at work? Perhaps simply making others happy at work brings happiness to you. Being powered by happy doesn't come easy, but it does come with great rewards. The most important questions to ask yourself are: Can you be happy at work? Is being happy feasible given the culture in which you work and the boss you have? If the answer to these questions is no, the best solution is to change your current situation and find happiness in a workplace where it is possible to be happy. Answering no to these questions and deciding to make changes in your life doesn't mean you have failed; it means you are succeeding in finding the most important characteristic in work (and life): being happy.

EXERCISE: BE HAPPY!

I hope the many personal stories I have shared about myself and those close to me have made you think about changes you can make to live a happier life. As a self-proclaimed happiness expert, I certainly hope you can benefit from my advice.

Remember, sometimes it takes work. Sometimes it requires you to make hard changes in your life. But in the end, the happiness you find will be worth it.

I'd like to end with one last exercise to encourage you to reflect on what you will take from these tips and apply to your own life. What is your plan to increase your happiness level at work? What will you do differently?

My goals in achieving a more fulfilled and happier life at home and at work are as follows:

_____

_____

_____

_____

As we end our time together, my wish for you is that your life is full of smiles, laughs, nice words, hugs, and bountiful joy every day.

ACKNOWLEDGMENTS

The opportunity to share my passion for happiness with others came about through the support of a few special people. Many thanks to my agent, Cynthia Zigmund, for her tremendous coaching and advice, and for believing in me. Her wonderful guidance has helped me realize my dream of writing this first book. I would also like to express appreciation to Ellen Kindle and Rebecca Rissman for their help in editing. The efforts and partnership of these individuals helped make the experience of writing my first book amazing.

It's also worth noting that I am not silly enough to think I could achieve true happiness on my own. The gifts of loving family and friends cannot be underestimated. Most importantly, my faith in God has sustained me through times that caused me to question whether I would ever be happy again. Many religious faiths espouse the principle of reciprocity, which means that real satisfaction in life comes only when you treat others as you want to be treated and pass your own special gifts and talents on to others. Fulfillment really does come when you "do unto others as they would do unto you."

REFERENCES

Bombeck, Erma. *Eat Less Cottage Cheese and More Ice Cream: Thoughts on Life*. Kansas City, MO: Andrews McMeel, 2003.

Chudler, Eric. "Laughter and the Brain." *Neuroscience for Kids*, January 22, 2009. http://faculty.washington.edu/chudler/laugh.html.

Emerson, Ralph Waldo. *Success, Greatness, Immortality*. Whitefish, MT: Kessinger Publishing, 2007. First published 1881 by Houghton Mifflin.

Haidt, Jonathan. *The Happiness Hypothesis: Finding Modern Truth in Ancient Wisdom*. New York: Basic Books, 2006.

Jeffers, Susan. *Feel the Fear and Do It Anyway*. San Diego: Harcourt Brace Jovanovich, 1987.

Levin, Miles. "LevinStory." *Carepages.com*, August 2007. http://www.carepages.com/carepages/levinstory.

McFerrin, Bobby. "Don't Worry, Be Happy." *Simple Pleasures.* Los Angeles: Capitol Records, 1990.

Ono, Yoko. "Beautiful Boy." *Double Fantasy.* Los Angeles: Geffen, 1980.

Patterson, Kerry, Joseph Grenny, Ron McMillan, Al Switzler, and Stephen R. Covey. *Crucial Conversations: Tools for Talking When Stakes Are High.* New York: McGraw Hill, 2002.

Peale, Norman Vincent. *The Power of Positive Thinking.* New York: Ballantine Books, 1996. First published 1952 by Prentice-Hall.

Pearsall, Paul. *The Last Self-Help Book You'll Ever Need.* New York: Basic Books, 2005.

Post, Stephen. *Why Good Things Happen to Good People.* New York: Broadway, 2007.

Seligman, Martin E. P. *Learned Optimism: How to Change Your Mind and Your Life.* New York: Free Press, 1998. First published 1991 by Knopf.

Washington, Ned, and Leigh Harline. "When You Wish Upon a Star." *Pinocchio.* Los Angeles: Walt Disney Records, 1940.

ABOUT THE AUTHOR

The Backstage Studio, Dublin, Ohio

Beth Thomas serves as executive vice-president and managing director of Sequent Consulting and is responsible for the overall success of the consulting practice. She also leads the organizational development practice, where she specializes in designing and leading transformational training and organizational design. She has twenty-five years of experience helping organizations through major transformations, such as mergers, acquisitions, and organizational changes.

Prior to joining Sequent, Beth was senior vice-president and head of retail training development and planning at

JPMorgan Chase. Before that, she worked at Limited Brands in Columbus, where she created and managed the retailer's Enterprise Learning Center and its service management practice. She has also worked for the international brokerage firm Fritz Companies, Inc.

Beth is currently on the board of directors for the American Red Cross's Blood Division and is a frequent national speaker. Her professional work has been recognized with national awards and in several nationally circulated magazines and newsletters. She is also a contributing editor to four books: *On Demand Learning*; *Implementing eLearning*; *Learning Rants, Raves and Reflections*; and, most recently, *Lies about Learning*.